All for the Love of Great Danes

Patti Dammier

iUniverse books may be ordered through booksellers or by contacting:

iUniverse
1663 Liberty Drive
Bloomington, IN 47403
www.iuniverse.com
844-349-9409

ISBN: 978-1-6632-6917-1 (sc)
ISBN: 978-1-6632-6918-8 (e)

Library of Congress Control Number: 2024924897

Print information available on the last page.

iUniverse rev. date: 12/27/2024

All for the Love of Great Danes

In memory of Allie, my wonderful companion

Contents

Introduction

This story compiles all of my special experiences with eight Great Danes. The decision to specifically write about them came to me because I realized how importantly they altered my life. They created the story because as I continued writing about the horses with the fiction stories about *Got Carrots? Rescued Horse*, finishing five books that were all about my adventures with horses, and the nonfiction book *All for the Love of Horses,* it became clear that the Great Danes, even though there was a period without their wonderful companionship, were a big part of my life. The Great Danes increasingly became important as they were included in life's events, especially beginning with the steady timeline that started with Irma in Germany, Tiki in Spain, and then Misty and Sebastian to continue with Harley, Henry and Allie, and now the puppy Sharlie. There hasn't been time on this farm without Great Danes…it has been wonderful. They have steadily supported me as I handled each of life's losses…they were quietly there. Each breed finds its niche and the Great Danes fit perfectly with mine. They're wonderful companions to horses with their easy-going character.

The Great Dane story tells how each positively transformed my life…this is their tale.

The Beginning

This story began over forty years ago in a small German village that had one of the largest chicken farms in the state of Hessen, but now continues on another farm in America. As I sit on the ATV parked on the back green field of the thirty-three acres now a horse farm, the view is a beautiful sunny day—quiet but somber— because someone is missing. For almost eight years this ride along the back fields was a happy, fun, joyous trip each day as the two of us raced over the fields, checking to see who or what had been there the previous night. What were the beavers doing over by the small pond at the corner of the field? What animal took a drink from the machine-dug canal that had been excavated at the farm, which has been a dairy farm for over 150 years? Looking over at the wetland on the other side of the canal, several ducks landed on a section of the field that still had water. They felt safe now that duck season has ended. Overhead, the resident eagle, perched on its favorite tree during the day, is now circling the field hunting.

Every view is a reminder of the happy times of riding horses, driving carriages, and long runs for all the Great Danes who lived on the farm. Sitting on the ATV looking at the peaceful scene, the years come flooding in a rush of the memory of that first wonderful time in Germany and by chance becoming the mistress of my first Great Dane. I also think of the horses enjoying exercise on the beautiful green fields. It was a change from the serious work in the constraints of the arena and the freedom of safely riding in the open space but still safely contained with perimeter fencing if a rider lost their seat. The free horse would still be in the confines of the large, fenced property.

Watching the eagle leave the favorite high tree perch, I am reminded when two young horses arrived from Germany and were beginning their outdoor excursion: out of the safety of the walls of the arena rides. The corner of the field had a small section of tall evergreens. At the nearest tree to the green pastures was a tall tree that was the lookout for an eagle. It was the habitual perch because it afforded a perfect view of the rodents scurrying through the grass. Being aware of sharing this outdoor playground with all the animals living here, I paid attention to any sudden appearances that would frighten a horse.

The young horse named Pavie, short for Pavarotti, and I were on one of our first outings to the back field and walked to the edge of the small forest. Stopping by the large evergreen, Pavie and I stood as I let him look around. Everything was quiet as we both surveyed the surroundings. Without warning above our heads, the resident eagle took off in search of prey. Suddenly, Pavie was aware of something above him and turned his head awkwardly to see what was coming. We both looked up but what was easy as me tilting my head, Pavie clumsily twisted his head to the side to view what was over him. Straining to move his head to see, he lost his balance and quietly fell over on his side as I stepped off the saddle. It all happened in slow motion, and I stood next to Pavie, reins in hand, while he easily got up and looked as if he didn't know what had happened.

While living in Spain, a fellow dressage friend told me about her experience riding on the beach with one of her horses when a helicopter flew closely overhead. It was the first time I had ever heard about a horse quietly standing and falling over, so I was intrigued by her story and tucked it away as interesting. Thinking about her story, I now knew that horses could fall over.

Now sitting on my own farm in the US, I think back to a lucky turn of events. I wasn't to own horses on this German farm but my first Great Dane Irma. This is how it all began.

Irma

While teaching school for the US overseas education, I rented a beautiful old house on one of the largest chicken farms in the state of Hessen, Germany. In the small village where I lived, there was a German high school where local friends introduced me to another American teaching at this school. At this point in my career, I was interested in teaching methods and visited my new friend in her classroom. Even though my group was the beginning grades, I used the popular music of the day to motivate my students, so I was invited to play for my friend's high school class.

Living in an old German house on one of the largest chicken farms was quite an experience. Each day, I drove the lovely country roads of Odenwald to the larger city of Mannheim where the school was located among what was a typical American base. It was a contrast of two lifestyles.

Life is fascinating how it brings new adventures. My friend's German fiancé was finishing his doctorate at the University of Heidelberg and his academic advisor had a Great Dane he couldn't keep. A big farm, big house, and big dog needing a home rather than staying tied up in a dormitory made it all come together, and Irma became my first Great Dane.

Actually, it began on Long Island where we didn't have a farm but a large piece of property and always lots of animals, such as the usual dogs, cats, and even a goat, plus a bartered horse. My mother loved German Shepherds, so besides all the dogs and cats we rescued there was always a Shepherd. She kept me supplied with rescued cats and dogs. Loving animals was part of my growing up. It was easy to take care of Irma; she was well-behaved so as the new owner there were few problems. She was easy- going and loved all the Jack Russell terriers that had the full-time job of keeping the rat population in control. Irma and I, occasionally during our long walks around the farm, would visit the huge, automated chicken barns where we watched these remarkable terriers working. They amazingly would take on a rat twice their size and humanly in one second with a neck flip euthanize these disease-carrying interlopers. Irma would quietly stand there without interfering or even barking at the spectacle we watched. It was as if she knew this was their job and we were merely observers.

Irma constantly endeared herself to the whole family and especially the young ten-year-old Willie who often joined her while she sat on the steps of the old *"Fachwerk"* house that was a beautiful example of the traditional wood timber construction. This was almost true with one exception. A young child of the farm owner's sister named Monfried often visited. He was not well-behaved or disciplined. During his visits he often ran around the farm getting into mischief…unlike his hardworking relatives. He had to be constantly watched. When he visited, everyone had to keep a close watch that he didn't get hurt.

The whole family including extended relations ran this farm with hard work. Even though the thousands of chickens were automated from hatching to final processing, a process that only lasted a matter of months, there was much to do. One of the jobs was taking care of the giant incubators, which hatched the little chicks for the farm. This provided an interesting science experience for my class when Herr Seltmann provided me with several eggs ready to hatch from their sophisticated automated machine for our little plastic bowl with a lightbulb. We did the same procedure the large machine did by monitoring the temperature with the students dutifully turning the eggs. The class was amazed when the eggs began to crack, and shortly there were three fluffy chicks. This was one of the best science projects I can remember, and we kept the little chicks until it was time for them to return to the farm.

There were horses on the farm but at this time, I was more interested in skiing and teaching. Irma went on long walks with us up in the fields. The fields ran behind the main farm and there were scenic paths through a wooded area that finally opened to huge fields on the higher part of the farm. Irma loved these outings as she ran along, keeping sight of us. There was a stream that ran through the farm that had interesting smells of the animals that previously drank at the edge. She was obedient and came when called. This had to be exhilarating for a dog that had spent her younger life tied up in a room. A remarkable fact about these miles of farm is that the owner, Herr Seltmann, didn't own the rights to hunting or water. When we took our long walks during hunting season, we had to be aware.

On one such excursion when my friends were along, Irma was cavorting in an open field below where we watched on a hill above. She enjoyed jumping through the tall field grass. We watched as she leaped joyously in and out of the high meadow. It was a peaceful sight when suddenly shots rang out and we were now all aware of the hunters in the field below and their intent on the leaping, bounding Irma in the tall field grass. Immediately we called to Irma and our friend yelled in his loud male German voice for the hunters to stop shooting at our dog.

We've all heard the joke about the highway police pulling over a car with an animal tied to the top and listening to the proud hunter tell the officer about his deer that is identified as a cow. These moments were terror as these hunters thought Irma was a deer. They kept shooting as we ran toward the hunters, yelling and waving while closing the distance, yelling for them to stop. Finally, after what seemed an eternity to us, the hunters stopped shooting, turned, and walked away toward the nearby road on the far side of the field where their car was parked. Irma was safe and we all learned a serious lesson about hunting in Germany.

Irma lived a happy life riding around in a VW camper and sitting on the porch watching the farm life, which also included the security "watch geese". No one could enter the road to the farm without the attention of Peter, the head of farm security. He was so large he could only manage flying about three feet off the ground, but this was enough for him to chase cars going in and out of the farm. A clear memory is looking in the rear-view mirror to see Peter airborne following the camper each day as I left the farm to drive to school.

Doggies are infamous for eating the wrong things. Irma had a close call when she discovered a three-pound jar of jam and ate it all. Sugar is toxic to dogs and had she not been large, and if we hadn't gotten her to the vet in time, it would have been tragic. Again, the military veterinary clinic saved one of my animals and later in the future one of my horses (*All for the Love of Horses,* 2020). Irma was given the treatment/medicine she needed to save her life—immediately!

Later when I had an eye infection, my swollen eye was the size of a lemon. I went to the military clinic and was told to go home and take aspirin. When I came home, Herr Seltmann and his family saw my eye and they were horrified. They called their local family doctor, who came to the farm and administered antibiotics. Yes, family doctors made home visits! When I wrote a letter to the *Stars and Stripes,* the military newspaper, praising the help my Irma received and lamenting that I wished I could have received that assistance for a serious eye infection, a reply to my printed letter stated that if I had kept my mouth shut like Irma, I would have received good treatment.

Life was happy for Irma. She must have been relieved to not be tied up in the dormitory. Here she was riding around with me, sitting on her porch, or sitting inside on her large couch. We were always welcomed at the local *Gasthaus zur Krone* where Irma sat under the table and received a huge bone to take home. This local restaurant was also famous for many game dishes. Their sign still has symbolic wild game animals. During the time we visited it had a real boar hanging from the sign. Of course it had been prepared. There was a renowned butcher shop we also visited; the local community came from miles around to purchase high-quality meat, so Irma was the happy recipient of many gifts when we bought wonderful schnitzels. After all, the Great Dane was also known as a *"Metzgerhund,"* which means a butcher's dog.

Irma was always around someone, and she loved Willie because he arrived home from German school before I did. Even though he had chores to do around the farm there was extra time and Irma became his favorite. Irma would go with Willie, who loved the companionship of a dog that made no problems with anyone on the farm or the working dogs. It was perfect. Irma had someone to be with until I got home from work, which often was late. This relationship was wonderful for Willie because the farm was really isolated from the nearby town; he didn't have friends his age living close. Irma could go with Willie while he did his chores and play with him on the otherwise remote farm. Irma had truly found her dog's purpose for two people.

Farmers' markets were restaurants that offered the local fresh produce. They specialized in specific dishes typical to the farm. There was a local *gasthaus* that was famous for its wine and a dish called *"kochkase mit music."* It was simply a piece of bread that had this wonderful, locally made cheese with onions. Doesn't sound too special but this local dish is to die for. Since you had to hike to this restaurant it was a fun trip for Irma. She was well-behaved and so she could be off leash.

If you suddenly have a taste for this wonderful Bavarian dish, a typical recipe may be found at this webpage (Koch Kase Recipe - Hermann Missouri Wine Trail). Many German specialty shops sell quark, which is strained curdled milk and the basis of "kochkase".

As we hiked to the restaurant, along the road was a herd of grazing cows. Irma decided that this was interesting and wanted to take a closer look. She walked nonchalantly to get a closer vantage of this new type of animal she hadn't seen before. She was only curious and nonaggressive and not even barking, so we couldn't see any harm. The cows quietly, as if on cue, began to move and their intent could be seen. Irma still stood quietly looking at the cows when it became obvious that the cows were encircling the oblivious Irma. While they formed this large circle as if on command around the unsuspecting suspect, they now started to move the circle inward. Realizing the impending silent danger, I hopped the fence and yelled to Irma. Irma still didn't understand the quiet cow danger. Finally, as I approached, the cows recognized a potential superior leader and started to move away as Irma came to me, and we went back over the fence the way we came. One of the nice parts about Germany was that pets were welcomed even in hotels; all they would ask was if she was housebroken.

There was a day when things looked serious for Irma. but she had a fan club on the farm, and it turned out okay. Monfried was an eight-year-old who was always into mean mischief, because with a momma that was always yelling at him, he had to find someone to take it out on. Certainly, his name in German that means "man of peace" could use some alteration. Thank heavens their visits were infrequent. When I knew he was around, Irma was kept inside because I caught him tormenting her while she sat peacefully on the porch. I gave him my best teacher talk to no avail. The next time I caught him, Irma was observed warning him about her thin patience. Monfried couldn't stop. One day again he came with his stick, tapped her, and turned to run. This time Irma had enough of his torment and was faster. She quickly bounded off her porch and nipped him in the butt.

Momma was in hysterics, and this was going to be the end of Irma. The office was near the house in a square courtyard that had four buildings. I could hear the yelling in the office and thought this would have a bad end. Again, the thirteenth godmother of all things good entered. Herr Seltmann came and told me that Monfried learned a good lesson not to tease animals and was sent off to the local doctor…with his momma. Irma had only bruised him. Everyone knew that Irma had been wronged, so she was rightly vindicated.

Having acquired Irma by chance, I didn't know anything about the breed of Great Danes; she was a dog needing a home. An interesting fact was that we learned from the website "Deutsche Dogge" (https://www.doggen.de/en, 2019) that this breed originated in Germany. Primarily a German horse owner, and carefully following the breeds, my interest is now focused on learning more about the dogs who have been so much a part of my life.

We had a happy life on the farm with many long walks and outings. Irma was always there for me until one day I ran a short errand, leaving her on her favorite rug in the VW camper. When I came back twenty minutes later, she seemed sound asleep. When I opened the package of her favorite treats, there wasn't any response. Our favorite vet's office was nearby in Heidelberg, but I knew there was no use, so I drove back to her happy farm and the family helped me find a place for her final rest on the farm that she so loved.

Irma's Story

My owner received me as a present from a girlfriend who wanted to impress her boyfriend. He was one of the lead faculty members of Heidelberg University; a good catch. He had a doctorial student who became very distressed about how I was kept tied up in the dormitory area of the university. I really wasn't wanted and Ulrich, who became my protector, suggested that his fiancée had a friend living on a huge farm who would love to take over my care. It was so hard for me as a young dog to stay day after day with only an occasional walk. I was still young and couldn't control myself when they couldn't walk me, so I was punished for my mistakes.

A wonderful day finally came, and Ulrich arrived at the dormitory and put me in his car. I was scared but I trusted this kind man who always spoke softly to me. When he tried to pet me, I knew he wouldn't hurt the way that others did. Shortly, we were driving down the farm road and I could smell all types of wonderful aromas. We pulled up to a house and I was introduced to a nice lady who was quiet. She didn't rush to pet me because Ulrich told her that I was occasionally nervous with strangers.

It turned out I had a funny habit that when people were tentative about petting me, approaching with their hand above my head, I would be worried and growl. She was comfortable with animals and talked with Ulrich quietly while I stood there listening. Finally, I sensed everything was all right and leaned forward to touch her with my nose. She gently stroked my shoulder with kind words. I was overjoyed to meet her. I trusted that my friend wouldn't take me anywhere unpleasant. Ulrich had saved my life because they had discussed euthanizing me when he broke up with the girlfriend. That's when he decided he had to find me a home.

Coincidence is a strange thing. Because Ulrich's fiancée knew a friend who lived on a farm, the pieces came together to find a solution for me. This became the beginning of a wonderful life free on the farm. The only time I had to be on a leash was at the beginning of training to become accustomed to the farm. All the people on the farm were accustomed to animals, so I reacted positively to all of them…except one. The youngest family member became one of my best friends and took me all over the farm on his adventures. He thought I was cool because I was huge compared to the working dogs on the farm. They thought catching rats was their thing. I wasn't interested in rats. Actually, my breed hunted boars and large animals.

What a change in my life. I went from lying on a dirty mattress alone to sleeping on a clean bed or my own couch. After I learned to come when called, I was free except when we went to public places. When I had my first free run, I was ecstatic to use my long legs.

Ulrich loved visiting the farm and brought his fiancée, who worked in a German school nearby. Lois and my mistress were friends, so I saw them often. They loved all the historical places and Ulrich became our tour guide with all his knowledge. I also got to go on ski trips and loved running in the snow.

Life was perfect for a Great Dane until one day I decided to explore a large jar of jam that was left out. I ate the whole thing and was deathly sick when she found me. She rushed me to the military veterinary clinic in Heidelberg and they saved me. Otherwise, life was uneventful with many farm outings until I almost was shot. Again, it was my friend Ulrich who saved my life by yelling to the hunters who thought I was a deer.

I was calm and everyone loved me…well, almost everyone. There was one unhappy little boy who luckily only visited the farm occasionally. He was always in trouble and my young friend had to look after his cousin when he visited. There were times when his cousin had to help with chores, so he was on the loose. He would come to where I sat quietly on the porch and tease me with a stick. One time my mistress caught him and scolded him not to tease me. He never listened to any adult and came back right near the porch when she was in the kitchen. He stealthily crept up on me sleeping and tapped me with the stick. I had enough and jumped up and nipped him in his butt. He let out a howl and everyone ran to see what had happened.

His mother wanted me dead, but the farm owner knew about his incorrigible nephew and sided with me. Afterall, I only gave him a little nip and it was only a bruise. This was the last time he ever bothered me again. Perhaps a lesson learned.

Years passed and I was now getting to middle age. I still went on all the excursions but was slowing down. My mistress didn't know too much about Great Danes because I was her first. She didn't know that they have short lives compared to my other relatives. So, one day on a short visit in the camper, I fell asleep.

Tiki

The time in Germany came to an end. A transfer to Spain was offered, so a large change began with another teaching position with possibilities for extending my philosophy about creating positive learning environments. This chapter intersects the book written about horses because several exciting new adventures were to transpire that would not only include Great Danes, but a scruffy terrier-type dog left for dead on a Spanish beach. Horses were now to enter a large part of my life and also learning to fly small airplanes.

Because of my mother's love for animals, all types of animals were being cared for—mostly cats and dogs. A small horse did come to live with us when my father took the animal in trade for work when he repaired their car. The horse was supposed to keep my younger brother occupied with taking care of a pet animal. As many parents who have made this error know, deciding on giving your child a pet without a tangible commitment generally ends in someone else taking care of the pet. That is exactly what happened. I took care of the horse. This was actually where my involvement with horses began but because of life's transitions, it never evolved until I arrived in Spain. It is at this junction that both dogs and horses came together in a wonderful period. Of course, there was a cat too…rescued by my mother and brought to Spain.

Once an animal takes over a piece of your soul you will never be the same. There is a scientific explanation about operant conditioning, which simply means that you have experienced positive reinforcement during your time with the animal and seek to repeat that happy relationship. There is, however, a silent communication between you and your animal that is hard to explain in words. People who haven't had that experience don't understand the depth of that relationship. Too many people believe that horses are for a type of work and dogs are messy. Unless someone has exposed you to another dimension of communication, since they can't use words, we can't communicate. We must simply learn a new language and be open to a new experience.

Being open to another experience is how Tiki came into my life. The memory of Irma was there tucked away secretly and when I saw an ad in the local American paper about a military couple offering black Great Danes, the contact was immediately taken. Their home was on the naval station where I taught school. We met and "Puppy" moved into my home surrounded by a five-foot-high cement wall.

These homes outside the naval station were rented to many of the military and civilians connected with the base. This lovely home shared a wall with my neighbor who was also a teacher. One of the reasons that homes had sturdy iron bars on windows and high cement walls was because robbery was high in these upper-level housing developments geared for tourists. This area overlooked the Mediterranean Sea and had many beautiful hotels. Tiki had a wonderful home, and I was totally safe from having my place robbed. The first thing was to install a doggie door to the entrance of the five-foot cement wall yard that would be her safe playground. She learned immediately how to push and swing gracefully through the opening. Even though the door was made large enough for a puppy to grow into a large Great Dane, it never had to be enlarged more. When she grew to full size she still gracefully glided through the door in one stride.

The house was about three blocks from a beautiful beach, so I began to take Tiki there when it was quiet. She was still small enough to carry, being about twenty-five pounds. She was learning very quickly to walk on a leash and eventually was so well trained on voice commands that I was able to take her free with the horses. This section of beach was quiet and didn't have the commercial usage as the hotels further down the beach. We would walk about two blocks to an opening. This day I had a large water bucket with me because it was warm. As we passed the last sections of houses that were right on the beach and turned off the road and onto the sand, two Rottweilers came tearing out and were bearing down on us. It was clear they were after Tiki. There are split seconds to change evil into good. Immediately I grabbed Tiki in my arms and began to swing the heavy cooler at the two now-attacking dogs. I yelled and screamed as loud as I could while swinging the water jug. Finally, in what seemed an eternity, I connected with a loud strike to his head, knocking him down. The dog let out a howl of pain and slowly got up. The other dog saw what had happened to his buddy and took off with the other limping behind. A man came running out to help. He told me this was a problem, and everyone was in fear of these two dogs; several children had been bitten. Having only been in Spain a short time, I was getting a new education about animals. I was to learn Chuck and his wife had retired and bought the nearby house. Unknown to me then, Chuck would help me again with horses.

Animals in Spain had a difficult time, but there were people such as a future friend to me and my horses who is still saving dogs. Many dogs were running all over in sad situations, which is how this poor puppy was found on the beach while walking Tiki. He came into our lives, and it seemed he wouldn't live, but again the wonderful military vet office helped. It was thought he had distemper and wouldn't survive but they successfully treated him. He now had a new home with a safe yard and was a large, growing friend. Our new friend was named Castaway, or Casta for short. He resembled a terrier breed called Griffiths. He was a complete opposite in attitude as the well-behaved Great Dane Tiki, who was taken everywhere, even with the horses. She would never venture more than a few feet away, coming obediently when called. Not the incorrigible Casta.

Once on a trail ride, we were walking along with the two horses and dogs when in the distance a dog was seen far, far away. Tiki stayed with us while Casta took off to chase the distant dog. I told Tiki to stay with my future husband while I rode off to corral Casta. He was surprised I caught up to him and I jumped down from the horse next to him. He laid down as if to say you got me. Indeed, I did, and I lifted his small frame up into the saddle in front of me where I held onto him for the rest of our ride. Tiki and Casta had a safe yard during the day to freely run in and out of the house while I was at school teaching. When school was over it was off to visit the horses. I would only take Tiki because she would dutifully, quietly sit by the arena and watch me exercise the horses. Casta had to stay in the play yard for his own safety.

Spaniards as a group don't like dogs and often teach their children to kick them, especially in the rural area where I lived in southern Spain. Spain has just as many cultural differences as we note in the US. This group also has a fear of anyone having a dog. Unfortunately, as in the case of the Rottweilers, they are trained to attack, so dogs primarily have this fear position. This is changing and more pampered-type pets are becoming usual. Since dogs typically guard houses, I never had the house robbed as did my fellow neighboring teacher who shared one wall with the house.

One day while standing in the kitchen where I had a view to the back door and walled yard, Tiki got my attention with a loud bark and dashed out the doggie door. Danes don't bark loud unless it is important. At once I focused my attention on Tiki who made several bounds and now was standing up over seven feet tall and looking over the cement wall. The next shock came when I saw she was staring at a face who promptly yelled in Spanish and could be heard falling on the ground. I quickly ran out to see who was on the other side of the wall. Two figures could be seen hastily running off in the vacant overgrown lot behind the house, screaming at each other as they ran…probably to the typical get-away vehicle parked on the next street waiting to carry the loot away. This was the typical robbery tactic. Because they were able to continually take my neighbor's stereo equipment and grabbable items, they thought this house right next to it would be an easy mark. All these years later, I still see Tiki standing on her hind legs face to face with that robber, letting out her ear-piercing woof right in his face. He's probably still telling his grandchildren this story… but a different version.

Tiki went to the stables where I rented two stalls at the Osborne summer home overlooking the beautiful water. She stayed dutifully sitting in the yard watching as I practiced in the arena, which we called the sand pit. Casta stayed home safely in his quiet backyard because he couldn't be trusted. The unsavory relative who "rented" the large house at the far end of the property overlooking the Mediterranean didn't like the fact that his uncle the famous wine maker rented part of his property to us and several Spaniards from Seville who were racing horses on the beach. It was important that we remain unseen to this nasty human. Andreas the caretaker also told us about him because he didn't like him at all. He was there as a free-loading relative and had Andreas playing the part of his servant. All Andreas wanted was to live quietly in the little caretaker's house at the front of the property near the stables. In the heyday of the winery the owner would have lived in the large house overlooking the water and Andreas would have taken care of their horses.

Finding hay was always a priority so a trip was made to a local farm where we could pick up our bales from the field. This was a great opportunity to take Casta with us because no one would be around…or so we thought. It was fun as we drove the blue Ford truck around the field picking up hay. Tiki stayed close when suddenly in the far distance, way on the other side of the field, a farmer herding sheep with his dogs was yelling at us. There was Casta in the middle of the sheep causing his usual mischief. We quickly drove over and scooped up the recalcitrant Casta and made many apologies to the farmer. Casta was always contrite when easily caught…as if he knew.

As described in my book about horses, we were always under duress to find new stables. Through my dressage coach, we became friends of a Spanish family in Arcos where I drove every day after school to ride not only my own horses boarded there but help train three of their stallions. They had a fantastic stable manager named Pepe who managed all the breeding and horse care. His whole life was taking care of the farm. We were discussing this dog we had who we couldn't trust to be free. Pepe said to bring him the next time. I did, and I warned Pepe not to let him out of his sight. Pepe didn't heed any of my suggestions. A week passed before we returned to Manolo's farm to see Casta following Pepe obediently. We asked him if Casta had run off or gotten into mischief. No, not even once. Casta was in love with Pepe and Pepe, who didn't have any pets, made a bond with him. The heartwarming book *A Dog's Purpose* described it all. Casta was rescued to give love and happiness to Pepe (2010).

Time marching on to new chapters leaves us with happy memories. The happiest time for Tiki and me was running on the beach. My mare loved Tiki and I think Tiki thought that she was part horse. Tiki learned this fantastic trick of jumping to tap my hand and we finally got what is one of my favorite horse and dog photos. This was the end of a chapter but made possible the next wonderful time with horses and Danes. I knew that the personality of a Dane was a perfect match with horses. Danes are not chasers, they don't have to be taught that horses are their buddies, and they can give a great back rub. This was my first time having both horses and Danes, which opened the future door when the time was right to have my own farm and have the ability to protect my animals.

It was time for another life change. This time I was assigned to a pilot school project in Zaragoza, Spain. Ernie, who I would soon marry, was assigned to Germany at an aeronautical university but would be teaching classes at the air force base in Zaragoza. This is where life became complicated as Ernie commuted between Spain and Germany, and I finally got a transfer to Germany. It is in Zaragoza where I met another animal lover, Maria Victoria, who not only loved dogs but horses also. She was to help me get my horses to Germany during the Barcelona Olympics' equine horse quarantine.

This is where the chapter about Great Danes comes to a temporary close with the loss of Tiki through the evil intent of the despicable man named Lorenzo, who lived in the Osborne summer home. I couldn't get her to the vet in time to save her. My dear friend Maria Victoria still to this day fights against the cultural cruel insanity against horses and dogs, which she says is becoming much better with people having family pets. She and her mother were saving dogs in Spain when we first met at a time when dogs were primarily only used and trained to be aggressive.

This next period is totally without Danes; it became too difficult to have the place to protect them until we arrived on the farm in America. These following years were the time with horses while living in Germany. Even though we had bought a home with a beautiful yard, because of our heavy work schedules with boarding horses and traveling weekends, having a dog wasn't practical. We just couldn't think about having another Dane, even though Germans love their animals, as seen in restaurants and hotels.

So, it wasn't until much later that the Great Dane story continued once again. This time it was because of the horses that the saga began back in the US with the conversion of a century-old dairy farm of thirty-three acres.

Tiki's Story

There was a happy beginning with five beautiful puppies, and I was one. We were all growing larger and since my family lived in a house on a military base, they couldn't keep so many dogs. It was advertised in the military paper that I was a black Great Dane. The paper was hardly published when a schoolteacher on the base answered the ad, and I was on my way to a new life.

We arrived at a cute house with its own backyard. Right from the beginning I was free with my own run of the house and high, cement-walled yard. Eventually I even had my own doggie door, so when she was at school, I'd have my own safe play yard. She was an animal lover and soon there was a bedraggle dog that became my playmate. He was kind of fun but not so well-behaved. He got to stay at home when she went on outings because he had his own mind. I always wanted to please her, so I got to go everywhere.

There was one time on our first outing when I was just a little puppy…well, Great Danes really are never little even when puppies, but she could still carry me if needed. We went to go for a walk on the nearby beach when two horrible snarling dogs ran out and were going to take me away. She started yelling and swinging something when suddenly, they howled and ran away. She was like my mother who never let anyone bother us.

I steadily grew larger and when I stood on my hind legs, I was over seven feet tall. My life was happy going on walks and being free in my house and play yard. I could run outside anytime using my doggie door. One day while she was in the kitchen, I heard something in the backyard. I leaped through the door and stood on my hind legs to see who was there. I came face to face with a man and gave my largest bark...right in his face. My mistress was alerted and turned to see this man who was going to climb over the wall. My instinct told me he wasn't good. I could hear him yelling as I had scared him off and protected our home. She was very pleased with me.

Shortly thereafter I was taken on an outing and introduced to large animals that were calm when I approached. They smelled different but I assumed they were a different version of me. They lowered their heads and sniffed me and I sniffed back. She then patted my head and brought one of them out in the big yard. I sat quietly and watched, never barking or chasing as they ran around with my mistress.

After I became trained to come, I was allowed to walk alongside these animals. She called me and I quietly walked along, following the large animal. This became great fun as I learned to run alongside them, and we would go to the beach when there weren't many people. What a life. I could run just as fast as these long-legged friends. They were my friends and treated me with respect and no fear. Well, I was well-behaved. She even taught me a trick to jump up and tap her hand. My friend wasn't afraid when I did this trick. She knew me because I walked around the place where she lived while my mistress was busy there moving things around. My life was a wonderful adventure of running with these large animals and living in my house with a safe backyard. No one ever tried to climb over our wall.

Life continued happily and I went everywhere because I would sit quietly and not bother anyone. The place where we visited the large animals, however, had some unfriendly people not like my mistress; they didn't like dogs. I never did anything to frighten anyone because I had never been hit, so I trusted everyone. When some meat was secretly left where I rested, I didn't think about not eating it. My mistress noticed I was sick and tried to get me to her military vet's office nearby; it was too late.

New Farm—New Great Dane – Misty

After the big transition of selling our German home, we were faced with a decision of where we would live. Ernie was offered three different positions with the university. Besides being his best option near one of the biggest aviation industries, it was the only place to buy a farm for a reasonable price. While I was selling our German home, Ernie spent his spare time checking out real estate agents, and riding around the area looking himself. When one of the agents we met appeared in four-inch heels to help us find a farm, we knew we had to find somebody else; enter Peg, who specialized in farm property. She arrived in sturdy hiking clothes, so we knew we were off and running…literally. Peg showed us every available farm property in the area. While I took a short vacation to return and join Ernie, I still hadn't sold our German home, so I had to return to Germany and leave Ernie to try and find a farm. And he did. While driving around, he saw a small sign attached to a tree, with an ad to sell over thirty-three acers of land—no house but an old barn and rustic silo.

Peg did her magic and we now owned acres of beautiful farmland with a barn and silo. This turned out to be the luckiest possibility with quickly finding a prefab home that looked like the floorplan of the German home, while also keeping the taxes down because an indoor arena was in the plan. With two quickly built stalls in the large, old barn for the horses that traveled from Germany, everything was going smoothly. When one of my dressage students wanted me to attend her jumping lesson, we arrived at a nearby farm. We were walking to the barn when out of the doorway walked a beautiful Great Dane. My heart stopped and I froze on the spot. A piece of memory unexpectedly flooded my thoughts as I remembered Irma and Tiki. Suddenly, my life wasn't complete as I recalled happier times and how much I missed their company. The owner told me that his Dane had a hearing problem and was rescued from a Great Dane breeder nearby.

This time we had our own farm for horses and now the possible safety for a Great Dane. It was always our goal to stop having to find the next place to board; now we were living it. Soon enough I visited the nearby breeder, and she had an extremely shy merle-colored female that had been returned by the people who bought her. The sad part of Great Dane history is the fact that many are returned or sent to rescue because the owners find this is more time than they want to invest. They are lovely, clean, house dogs and even though they are well-behaved, they are too large for most homes. The breeder came to visit our farm and home before she would rehome this sensitive dog. Misty now became the first of a line of Great Danes that luckily came to live totally free on the farm.

When the weather was suitable for outside, Misty had a favorite large bush that she would hide under to survey the comings and goings on the farm. When the weather was inhospitable, she had her own couch. It was the large L-shaped couch we brought back from Germany. Misty didn't make friends the way the other Danes did by going in their stalls and getting backrubs but loved going along on the rides to the huge back field.

I've never had to teach either the horses or the Danes to walk with each other. Misty would run or walk along with the horses on the field exercise. Even though Great Danes are quiet inside and not inclined to bark much, they really do benefit from stretching their long legs. Actually, we call them one-bark dogs. They only must bark once in their loud deep voice to alert anyone. The breeder stayed in contact with us and was pleased when she visited and found how well the shy Misty was progressing. She thought that Misty might have a slight hearing problem that caused her to be overly timid. This was the perfect place because the farm was quiet with only us and the occasional adults who helped with the horses. It was a private farm, so we didn't have any boarders coming and going. The breeder was extremely content with this match for Misty.

Misty was affectionate and performed the usual Dane sitting on your lap and chairs the way a person would. Our new life was busy as Ernie had a full job as the aviation undergraduate program chair and teaching at all the extended centers connected with aviation businesses and the military education.

Life has a way of throwing a curve ball, so big changes are necessary. I was a fully certified Department of Defense teacher with a master's degree and an additional certificate in early childhood education. Washington State had a protectionist view of teachers coming from other states. My plan was to continue teaching at the elementary school level in our newly adopted state. I was overly qualified and had run a pilot research program for early childhood education. The best laid plans…. I stopped fighting the system and continued a doctorate program I had begun while in Europe. Looking back, it turned out to be an auspicious plan.

In fact, it all worked perfectly. After receiving my doctorate, I began teaching graduate research classes. Ernie and I began to collaborate on human factors research projects with Ernie the aviation content expert. I taught the students the research criteria and served as the chair for many graduate projects. While a member of the International Applied Behavior Analysis Organization, I presented several studies and was able to travel to Spain and China. Meanwhile, the farm had steady help to take care of everyone to fill in for our occasional absences. The farm was a perfect place. It also became home to several new horses that came from Germany and several foals born to the beautiful German Trakehner mare.

Misty had the comfort of a steady schedule. A wonderful opportunity came to pass when a colleague of Ernie who lived in Hawaii was being transferred to Alaska. She knew we had a farm and a Great Dane. Wouldn't we love to share our farm with another Great Dane? Yes, and so Misty was going to have a fun companion named Sebastian, another merle-colored Great Dane. Sebastian had to wait a short period until the warm weather cooled enough for him to fly from Hawaii to Seattle. Since Sebastian was a large, two-year-old dog, he needed the large space of the pressurized service. We waited excitedly for Sebastian's flight date.

Misty's Story

My life started as one of four puppies on a Great Dane breeding farm where we had the run of the place. My owner spent all of her time cleaning and taking care of us. We lived in her small house that she polished every day. The day came when I was purchased by a family who thought it would be wonderful to own a Great Dane. They had no idea about what it takes to raise a Great Dane. We remain immature until fully grown at about two-years-old. They were not motivated to keep up with a large puppy. I was summarily returned to the breeder and thankfully not sent to a shelter. It wasn't a happy time because they yelled a lot. I was very sensitive and when I found myself back at the farm where I was raised, I was overjoyed and knew I would be safe again. Most of my time was spent hiding and my owner was worried about me. A lady who she knew came to look for a dog to rescue because she definitely was not going to sell me again. After I came to my new home, it was different being allowed to be free in the yard and in the house. I had my own couch.

It was nice because my earlier owner came to visit to make sure I was happy. She knew I had become extremely shy. It was thought that I might have a slight hearing problem because my brother was totally deaf. It was a wonderful change, and I had a secret place where I quietly sat to watch the comings and goings. There was a large bush situated next to a small pond that was made into a flower garden. The large nearby bush had a perfect cave-like shape that I could sit in and see everything happening in the courtyard. Life was perfect...well, almost perfect until one day to my surprise right in the middle of the courtyard my mistress had a large dog!

I watched secretly as this beautiful, large, merle-colored dog, like me, proceeded to run around and around the house and barn, then without warning came to stop near the onlookers. Wow, that looked like fun. Without warning he discovered me hiding under the bush watching. He only stared so my fear vanished, and I decided to get closer. He stayed quietly looking at me as if to say, "It's all right, I want to be friends." I continued to move closer out from the bush and he stayed, kindly looking at me. I knew most of my Great Dane friends at my previous farm were affectionate and loving. Since he appeared the same way, I gathered my courage and walked up to him. He greeted me as a long-lost friend, enthusiastically wagging his tail.

This changed my life. I was content that my mistress was kind and gentle but having another friend opened up new activities because he was vastly more self-confident. Now, I followed my friend everywhere, safely on the horse-fenced part of the farm, unafraid. We shared the L-shaped couch, our food, and free outings in the safe confinement around the house and barns.

Sebastian

The day finally came, and we drove to the airport with the pickup truck, so we had room to bring Sebastian's large crate home. His owner was with us. When we picked him up at the Alaska cargo depot, he felt reassured to see a familiar face. The short ride to the farm delivered the large crate to the middle of the courtyard where his owner opened the crate and Sebastian stepped out and sat in front of his owner, looking as if to say, "All right, are we going for a walk?"

Sebastian was always walked on a leash by her older son who was now headed to college. Sebastian was accustomed to never going anywhere accept on a leash because there wasn't any place he could run free. We stood together with Sebastian looking around and being told by his owner to go run. He took a few tentative steps and then realized he was free to run. It was wonderful to see him run around the house several times, returning to sit in the courtyard with us. The farm is horse-fenced with five-foot-high special mesh horse fencing; we knew he was safe.

Later on, Ernie's colleague demonstrated her true personality in many ways, not only with this beautiful dog but with the university. She didn't want the responsibility of a dog that would be inconvenient with the new position. Since he really belonged to her son who wasn't going to be able to care for him, she had to find a way to rid herself of this problem and anyone else she used to help her get ahead that was in her path. It was lucky for Sebastian that he found his next loving family.

During all of this excitement Misty had been watching from the safety of her special bush. Sebastian now noticed her and quietly looked in her direction. Since he was so quiet, Misty decided she should come out to see her new friend. They were now nose to nose with tails wagging that assured us what we all knew. The two became inseparable and shared everything, including the L-shaped couch. It was such a happy moment for Misty; she became much more outgoing with her new friend. It was a match made in heaven.

We were lucky to have a vet who could handle two Great Danes visiting her office. She was the colleague of our wonderful horse vet. She had a side door to one of the examining rooms, so it was easy to get their necessary visits in one trip. It wasn't that they were aggressive with other dogs, but even though they were well-behaved it was distracting to have this pair of dogs weighing over a hundred pounds each walking into the waiting room, no matter how quiet they were. The Loving Care Clinic was perfect in every respect during the time of Sebastian and Misty. The drive to the vet worked because, luckily, there weren't any problems that needed quick attention. Our quiet thirty-minute drive was increasingly becoming longer with the growth in traffic. In fact, the hardly traveled road in front of the farm became a shortcut route to bypass traffic from a major highway. It is during this period that we installed an electric gate for security to ensure no one left the main gate open. It is a blessing we installed this high-tech gate before events worsened, and someone left the gate open, or an animal walked out on what was now becoming a major road.

Life on the farm expanded to the two original horses brought from Germany, Xierxo the Portuguese Lusitano and Fanfare the German Trakehner mare, with two German Trakehner geldings. It was a full house with occasional students boarding their horses with me. It occurs to me reviewing the timeline back to Germany and the first Great Dane that this would be the goal: both horses and Great Danes. The involvement with horses appeared to be more planned than the Danes but they really were part of our life. It was only during the German period that it didn't seem fair to have a dog sitting home alone, and since the unfortunate episode in Spain I didn't want to consider having a dog unless we had our own farm.

Misty and Sebastian were free to roam the horse-fenced property in total safety. The only people who came on the farm were animal friends. My mother came for a visit and the farm became more populated. As I mentioned, my mother, who lived back east on Long Island, was always rescuing animals. Her latest rescue was an active mixed Labrador and Shepherd mix that wasn't working out too well. Dreyfus, as he was named, was an active type who really needed a job herding. My mother's property wasn't fenced well enough to keep him contained so she built him a kennel. He proceeded to climb up the ten-foot kennel wall. She persisted and took him to a special dog trainer who said he was smart but couldn't stop him from aggressively chasing your feet. He didn't bite but it was so unnerving that even that dog trainer gave up. Dreyfus then had a chance to become a drug dog and worked great with the trainer who said he was one of the best dogs he had trained. The problem started with the kennel staff who he intimidated with his foot chasing fetish. Again, Dreyfus flunked out and this time it was drug school. The reader knows who arrived along with my mother…Dreyfus.

We hoped that the well-behaved Danes would be a good influence on Dreyfus, but thirty-three acres wasn't enough space. One day my farm neighbors called to say that they thought they just saw Dreyfus heading down the main highway that passed both our farms. They recognized him from the time they cut hay on our property. We quickly drove toward their farm and there was Dreyfus running along the road. I stopped and he happily got in. What happened next doesn't make any behavioral sense. There was a gate that closed the front part of the property from the back fields. It was usually left open because the Danes would never go unless with us. Not Dreyfus. One day I caught him running down this lane to the back field. He turned to see me. "You want to go…now go and you can't come back." I started yelling at him and threw rocks at him, chasing him further down the lane. Every time he turned to come back, I threw a rock and chased him away. I kept chasing him until he was into the hay field. I can't say this was one of my well-thought-out training plans. Surprisingly, this had a different ending.

Later on that night, who was sleeping in one of his favorite places in the barn? Dreyfus. I gave him his normal dinner at the time we fed the horses. What happened next was amazing. Dreyfus never ran away again and became more social with the Danes. Each dog breed has its own characteristics, and this disparity became obvious that Dreyfus was different. Things became much easier because I didn't have the dread of Dreyfus running away and having to tell my mother bad news. I was under constant stress every time he had gone off.

This wasn't the only problem that had to be solved. Another nearby farm called to tell that there was a coyote in my pasture chasing my horses. There are problems with coyotes but normally they go after cats. Sure enough, I went to the pasture and Dreyfus was chasing the horses. His slightly yellow color made him look just like a coyote.

In contrast, Misty and Sebastian only wanted to be with their humans. I knew that Great Danes were a good choice with my horses. They were also excellent in trying to keep Dreyfus in check. Especially Sebastian, who was a large male and had started to reprimand Dreyfus when he was chasing the horses. Sebastian was standing at the fence giving orders but Dreyfus, acting as the typical obnoxious teenager, ignored him. I began to realize if I heard Sebastian give his one bark alert that it meant Dreyfus was up to something. Sebastian became the barnyard cop and babysitter.

Misty and Sebastian were house dogs. When it was freezing during winter, they had coats to be outside for any length of time because they have no undercoat. Dreyfus with his Shepherd-type fur had a good coat. The barn was his place, and he had several cozy places in the stacked hay. He could also keep watch on any intruder comings or goings. It was his territory and he guarded it possessively. Several times when it was a colder evening, we tried to bring him inside. He would begrudgingly come in and stay on the little bed we had for him, which he rarely used. When we went out to do anything with the horses, he would go with us to the barn and not want to leave. We'd have to lead him back to the house. He had established the barn as his territory.

Misty was quietly affectionate and was the quiet spirit that was around without noticing her. She was wonderful around the horses because of her easy-going manner. Misty was much more fragile than Sebastian and began to have some health issues. It is similar to finely bred horses, Danes have potentially many problems and are noted for their short lives. Not really good odds but two of the seven Great Danes lived to thirteen years old. Misty, as much as my vet at Loving Care Pet Clinic tried, was lost to kidney failure quietly in her sleep.

Our attention now turned to Sebastian, who stopped eating and stayed on the couch. I now needed a vet that was closer because with the care of the horses there wasn't much time to make the trip to Loving Care Pet Clinic. I questioned Dr. Russell she said there was an independent vet close to me. It was decided for Sebastian's sake to get a closer vet. It was how we found Dr. Thomas, who discovered there was nothing physically wrong with him. He couldn't continue not eating. Nothing we offered him was working. I went on the internet and found that the Idaho rescue had a female Great Dane. This is how the story went. This next part is from my book *All for the Love of Horses* and how we found Sebastian his next companion (2022). This was an important lesson about how deep unspoken communication is. We assume because there are no words that nothing has occurred, but the silent presence is powerful.

Sebastian's Story

Suddenly I became the beloved dog of a teenager living in Hawaii. He was lonely because he was an only child. His mother was nice but was totally distracted by other things. The place where we lived had limits to where I could be free to run but my young owner was very athletic and took me with him for runs on the beach every day. I was well behaved and quiet inside as all of us are.

Life continued with the same pattern and my young friend was getting taller, just like me. One day they put me in a box, and I was scared, but the lady seemed to be in charge of what was happening. I was in a dark place for several hours when my box ended up in a strange place, but the lady was there talking to me. There was another ride, but this time I could see and smell things. My box was set down and the door opened, which allowed me to step out. I was surprised to see not only the lady but other people who quietly stood looking at me. I sat patiently, not afraid because I recognized the lady who often fed me. She wasn't putting me on a leash but telling me to go and run. Standing there not knowing what to do, the people kept urging me to go and run. In an instance I knew I was free to go and run just the way I did with my young friend on the beach. I took off and ran around the house three times and returned to sit next to my waiting friends.

In an instant I became aware of being watched, and I noticed a pretty-looking merle like me staring at me. I knew at once she was just like me. She was beautiful and very ladylike sitting there. I decided to be gentlemanly and not frighten her. It was the correct move because she now moved out from under the bush and took a few steps toward me. I wagged my tail to show my appreciation. Suddenly we were nose to nose. She smelled so nice. She was shy but took me inside to show me where we lived. I felt comfortable right away. Two of the people owned this wonderful place and fed me my first meal in my new home.

This was a wonderful home and I never had to be run around on a leash. I had a new friend, and we were happy every day running around the farm together. We went on outings with the long-legged animals, running to our hearts' content. My new friend and I both went to the vet, and I started to become aware that my friend had a problem. My mistress spent many hours taking her to the vet and giving her medicine. We slept together in their bedroom on our beds or on our favorite couch. When we went to sleep in the bedroom, I noticed that she didn't climb into her bed but stayed on the rug near me. We fell asleep. I didn't understand but the next morning, she didn't get up. I couldn't know what had happened or even what was being done. All I knew was that she wasn't there, and I was lonely. I stopped caring about anything. My mistress tried to get me to eat with all types of tasty meals…I didn't care. She took me to the vet, but it was no use.

My mistress finally took me on a car ride with the person who was always with her. He was kind too. We arrived and strangely I was put on a leash and led to a grassy spot. My heart leaped into the air because in front of me was another that looked like me, only in another color. My life flowed back into me and I felt like myself again. I loved my mistress dearly, but I became used to having a friend such as myself. She knew I needed a companion.

This time I took charge and showed my new companion the farm. She was much more outgoing than my previous quiet friend. My friend was quicker to become upset than me and she had to have my mistress teach her to become calm around people. I had a wonderful life as a younger dog but her first home made her afraid. I saw her get very upset several times. She was great fun, and we were free to run and play.

I even took her on a long trip to the back of the farm where we ran around checking out different smells. Even though I had a beautiful girlfriend I was still a young male at heart and looking around. My mistress was worried and came to find us. Because of her bright color she found her right away. My merle color allowed me to sneak home through the tall grass without being seen. I made believe I was home the whole time by sitting calmly on the porch. They were only worried about us, so we didn't get into trouble.

Harley

This is exactly how we found Sebastian a new friend and instantly restored his life. We realized that we had to find a companion for Sebastian. Finally finding a Great Dane rescue group in Idaho, the arrangements were made to visit their foster home in eastern Washington.

The appointment was made and Sebastian was ensconced comfortably in the back of the SUV and we proceeded to drive about three hours across Washington. At last, we reached the kennels where we were to meet a potential companion. After we met the owner of the kennel and Sebastian was introduced, we met a beautiful black-and-white harlequin Great Dane. She seemed somewhat subdued, but that is often the outcome of kenneling dogs. Everything was perfectly clean but to house so many dogs needed some schedule of exercise, feeding, and cleaning. It was decided that the new Great Dane, of about eighteen months old, named Harley, would be brought outside and we would take Sebastian to a meeting on neutral ground.

Unusually, Sebastian was put on his leash, and we walked to where the beautiful, alert, female Great Dane stood. If we had any trepidation about this meeting, it was over in seconds. The two tails beat happy rhythms as we now let them meet. The transaction was now made as Sebastian turned toward the SUV and Harley followed, pulling her handler along. Sebastian now jumped into the back and Harley followed. They settled themselves in the back of the SUV, as if they had known each other forever. The kennel owner for the rescue shelter stated the obvious that this seemed to be a perfect home for Harley.

After the several-hour trip back to the farm, it was time to feed horses and dogs. Harley has her place and Sebastian his spot on the L-shaped couch. We dished up their mostly home cooked meal of their dog meal with today's special stewed chicken done in my mother's old pressure cooker. Since then, I have one of the newer electric models with Teflon insert to cook, retiring my mother's well-used model. We put each of their dishes down and waited expectantly. Both Harley and Sebastian ate and we were greatly relieved. I called our vets to tell them the good news.

This was the beginning of a long and happy period on the farm. Sebastian became his predictable self and he and Harley were inseparable. The L-shaped couch had to be retired, and Chris, who has now been a close friend, helped me pick out a leather version. Why leather? Because in England where I spent a summer riding, they had a dayroom where all types of riding boots and doggies sat on several leather couches that were several years old. All they did to clean them was use saddle soap, like on the saddles and bridles. The salesman agreed with my account of buying a leather couch and said that the trick was to buy the correct grade of leather. He showed us several models, so a new leather L-shaped couch was delivered. Each dog had a section and we got to sit on the sides or in the extra chairs. Danes are famous for being chair sitters as several of the pictures show.

Chris, her husband, and a friend were visiting us as we all sat around with the TV on in the background. Ernie and I loved sailing but resisted buying a boat, even though we had sailed while in Spain. Our friends, who had recently retired, were working to refurbish an older boat with plans to sail to Alaska, so the talk was all about these plans.

The Danes were sitting on various laps when suddenly Harley leaped up, attacking the TV. We couldn't imagine what got her attention. It was the full face of a cowboy with a large hat. As soon as he was off the screen, Harley ran to the other side of the wall into the kitchen. She assumed that if he wasn't on the TV he must be in the kitchen. We were amazed but didn't think any more about it until a dear friend came to visit us all for a big, fun breakfast. Our friend had helped look after Misty, Sebastain, and the horses when we both had to be gone. He had a local business and was also a rancher who we had initially met when he did all the drainage work on the farm. Dave was a wonderful, trusted friend, so what happened next was upsetting.

All of our friends came and went with no formality, so when Dave walked up on the deck. We heard his boots as he came to the door and walked in where we were all having a wonderful breakfast. We were all exchanging happy greetings because he knew our friends also. Suddenly, Harley leaped up on him, growling. He luckily had his heavy rancher's jacket on. We all grabbed Harley and put her and Sebastian in the bedroom. We all calmed down enough to sit down and try to proceed with what was to be a fun breakfast. We were all in shock. We tried to figure out what had happened. It appeared that because of Harley's previous violent reaction to the cowboy on the TV, she made a direct connection to our wonderful rancher friend who was dressed the same with his hat. He had only come from feeding cows. It rains a lot in Washington and those hats are very handy, not only trendy.

The mood was somber as we tried to figure out what was going on with Harley. Definitely it was the hat because of her reaction to the TV. We finished the breakfast and Dave, who has been attacked by bulls, passed it off. It was a break in the trust of a good friendship. We had to work hard to restore it. Dave loved our family, horses, and dogs, and we loved him. It turned out all right and as long as Dave didn't have his hat on, things were okay.

Dave was to help me with a sick horse and drove us in his large rig to a famous clinic. Xierxo, my beloved Lusitano that was brought from Portugal, made it through colic surgery to live many, many years more. I wrote this story about all the wonderful people who stepped in at just the right time, and Dave was one of them. Chris and I were able to help him when he was recuperating from a heart attack when he was abruptly released from the hospital after four days and sent home without any assistance. I felt happy to repay Dave for all his kindness and help getting our farm started.

Piecing the story of the history of Harley's rescue timeline, she was sent from Texas to the Idaho rescue we think to save her life, because they most likely had some problems with Harley and cowboy hats. I had her tag from Texas. We can accurately know that she never bit anyone but rather was aggressive with pinching arms. This began a new challenge on the farm to make sure no one was wearing cowboy hats.

This was another test for me to retrain a dog using behavior modification that I expertly wrote about for horses. We had to keep our eyes peeled for Harley with certain men. She loved Ernie and all our friends. We had several horse friends and the husband of one of them decided to be a dog trainer and show Harley her place. He started to move his hands aggressively to make Harley do what he wanted. I was there and noted the hand cue that upset her. A new plan to get Harley to change her response to quick-moving hands was quickly developed. I'm pretty sure she was hit to punish her. There are so many more effective ways to deal with behavior, so now I was going to try this with a dog. I wrote extensively about the negative effects of controlling horses by striking them.

Briefly the plan was to change the moving hands to the command to sit. This went quickly as Harley was smart. Move the hands, sit, and treat. She learned this in days. Then I added move the hands, sit, treat, and pet with hand. I had noticed that anytime someone moved their hands near her she would flinch. Irma had a little of this flinching problem too. With horses, one can always tell if they're being struck for the same reason. This worked so well with Harley that she actually became annoying to a friend because the moving hand now meant getting pet and she'd push your hand to get pet.

This was perfect for me! Harley was pet as much as she wanted. Dave finally became friendly with Harley, but it was never the same as it had been with shy Misty. This is a perfect example of how one can train incompatible behavior.

This is a major difficulty with rehoming an animal if they have been handled roughly and those past cues are dormant. Fortunately, Harley's future was wonderful considering her rough beginning. Better to begin rough and end smoothly; this is exactly what happened. She became a wonderful loving dog who now occasionally bothered folks by pushing their hands to be pet. If she were tested by suddenly waving your hand quickly at her head, if you looked closely, you could see a tiny flinch—if you knew what to look for. Immediately she was pushing your hand to be pet.

Life on the farm was at a high point with contented horses and Great Danes. Both Harley and Sebastian went with us on the rides with the horses in the safety of the back fields. We started one of the German horses with a small cart so there was fun for the Danes to go along with the horses. It's most likely the reason that both lived to the age of thirteen. They followed the schedule of the horses to feed, rest, and exercise at specific times. Thinking back, we followed an exact schedule of feeding, quiet time, and progressive warm up before exercise with the horses. Harley and Sebastian fell into this schedule. The two were never out of sight until one day we went to look for them to find them nowhere on the front of the farm near the stalls and indoor arena. Maybe they took a walk to the back field, which was now tall grass waiting to be hayed. It would be possible for them to be there and not be seen, especially Sebastian, who was a merle color. Now, Harley with her white and black should stand out, even in the tall grass. Ernie and I took a walk to the back field looking for them, but we found no dogs. We couldn't figure out where they could be.

The farm, an old dairy operation, is divided by a deep canal that was used to water the upper fields during the summer. There were two crossovers to the field section of the opposite side of the canal. Maybe they went there. The whole farm is basically fenced but the front section is five-foot horse-fenced. I tacked up Pavie and rode out on the other section. When I began walking back, I discovered the loudly colored Harley walking back to the house. Sebastian wasn't to be seen. Harley and I walked back to meet Ernie. We were now worried and wondered if he could have walked out the back section where there is a perimeter road. We put Harley in the car and drove around to the back of the farm where a road led to the houses. No Sebastian. We worriedly drove back to the farm. When we drove up to the house, guess who was sitting on the porch? He was on the farm all the time and decided he would sneak back when he saw me with Harley. Who says dogs don't have a sense of humor?

Another mystery was the day we found Harley sitting on the front seat of our truck. The back sliding windows that opened to the bed of the truck were found to be closed. How could Harley have gotten into the front of the truck? The mystery was solved several days later when we observed Harley perform what seemed to be an impossible trick. I knew that Danes are talented jumpers as evidenced by the high jump of Tiki with my horse. We watched unbelieving as Harley, standing by the door of the truck, suddenly jumped through the open window of the driver's side door. And now she was seated just as the previous day on the front seat. Had we not seen this, no one could believe that a full-sized Dane could perfectly jump through that size of a window. I have watched the deer on the property effortlessly clear the high horse fences and Danes appear to have the same powerful hind legs and light bodies. Harley, Tiki, and the future Henry had the physique of a deer with jumping power. We occasionally watched deer that came on the farm as they easily jumped the pasture fences.

This was another incredible period on the farm and Sebastian and Harley both lived to the impossible Great Dane age of thirteen wonderful years. They had a perfect life running free and were well-behaved with the horses, which is how this Great Dane adventure had begun so long ago in Spain with Tiki running on the beach with the beautiful Andalusian mare Shenandoah. There were to be several other Great Danes on the farm and a pit bull, who I rescued when someone tossed him out of their car while I was driving back from picking up horse feed and groceries.

While driving along the forest that ran through the middle of the army base, a car came suddenly out of a wooded area with a dog chasing the car. I stopped as did another car because we saw what had happened. The other car that stopped were military and couldn't keep him, so he climbed into my front seat with some hamburger meat I took from one of the bags groceries to make him feel safe. He sat there on the passenger seat with his head soulfully resting on the middle console, looking at me. He seemed to know that he had been rescued. It was an amazing moment as he spoke his quiet gratitude and looked at me as we drove to his new home. Scooter was incredibly smart and his own dog. We now were faced with another rescue who wouldn't stay in the confines of the thirty-three-acre farm. But he became the friend of the next Dane.

Harley's Story

I was sold as an exceptional Great Dane—they even paid to have my ears clipped so they would stand up and look formidable. As soon as I took a dislike to being struck by a person wearing a cowboy hat, my life became difficult. Only growling and giving a pinch. I never bit anyone, but I was sent away to a rescue place for dogs. Suddenly I was shipped to the Idaho rescue, maybe because it was thought that I would forget how much I hated cowboy hats.

There wasn't enough room at the shelter, so I was sent to another in Washington State. It was a nice place, and everyone was so kind. There weren't any cowboy hats in sight, so I was well-behaved. No one knew about my past bad behavior. This place had other friends, but they didn't look like me. Then a wonderful thing happened, my handler put my leash on, and I was walked outside to a different place. What a surprise! There was a larger animal that looked like me that was walking toward us. I knew he was a friend because he wagged his tail. I could hardly wait to meet him. He touched my nose, and it was love at first sniff. He turned with his mistress, and I joyfully dragged my handler to a waiting SUV that had the back opened. We promptly jumped in. All the people standing nearby looked pleased; we were on our way.

I was introduced to my new home, and Sebastian, my new friend, showed me around. He shared his L-shaped couch, feed place, and all of his favorite toys. I never had to be on a leash and had lots of fun sitting on the couch with my mistress and all her companions. We were watching TV when all of a sudden one of those cowboy hats appeared and I jumped up barking and was trying to get him. They were all shocked and made him disappear.

Everything was wonderful. It was exhilarating to run around with my friend. What a life. But one day when she and several happy friends were sitting around the table, a large cowboy hat appeared suddenly while Sebastian and I were quietly sitting under the table. I was shocked and leaped out from under the table and jumped on this horrible, wicked person before he could hit me. They all jumped up and quietly took Sebastian and me to a quiet room.

Nothing bad happened to me. My mistress didn't even raise her voice and yell at me. The next day she started to wave her hands and I was told to sit. She at once gave me a treat. We did the same thing over and over.

One day one of her friends visited and was going to show me who was boss and started waving his hands around and yelling at me. I suddenly pinched his hand. I didn't want to get hit. My mistress saw this and told him immediately to stop moving his hands and took me to where Sebastian was sitting inside on his favorite couch. She continued our lessons by waving her hands, I had to sit, and getting a treat. After a while this became easy and I would immediately sit if anyone waved their hands at me. Shortly after I learned this lesson where she would move her hand suddenly and pet me on the head. The first few times I flinched but after doing this and I got treats and petted, I began to look to get petted by nudging someone's hand. Eventually, I became a little annoying by nudging people to pet me, but I never ever pinched anyone again. Nobody really minded the nudging and I got lots of hugs and petting.

Running on the farm with the long-legged animals that I loved was great exercise. I was over ten years old. This was extremely old for a Great Dane. My mistress was concerned and made an appointment with my favorite vet, Dr. Thomas. She explained that even though I was in great shape for an older Dane, my back legs were getting painful. Besides getting the medicine that I took easily, I was going to receive a treatment procedure. We went to the clinic several times a month and my mistress sat with me as she slid a small wand along my legs. I was much more comfortable for several years until finally I could hardly stand or walk. My mistress was so sad, and she tried so hard to help me keep going. She called a kind person I had seen many times on the farm helping my long-legged friends. I had my favorite blanket. He gave me something and I closed my eyes and went to sleep.

Henry

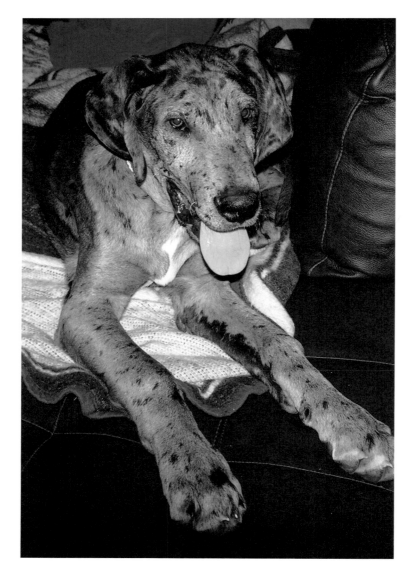

Henry was found on the internet by Ona, one of our helpers who not only loved horses but dogs as well. There was a picture of him in an empty room looking lonely. He was a purebred Great Dane but we later surmised he wasn't from a conscientious breeder. He had been given vaccinations but didn't seem as robust as the other previous Great Danes.

It was right around Christmas when we met the owners in the Safeway parking lot to take ownership of Henry. He seemed all right and was making a good adjustment when I noticed him lying on the couch, and I sensed something didn't seem right. I took his temperature and it was at the high side of the normal dog range. Our normal vet was not available because of the holidays, so I called our nearby twenty-four-hour emergency vet service and asked to bring him in. My sixth sense may have saved his life because he was at the beginning of a serious intestinal difficulty. He didn't have the problematic intestines that often twist yet but he needed immediate attention.

Having just Henry was now the first time in many years that there was just one Great Dane. There was of course Scooter, who taught Henry every bad habit he knew. The first thing he taught Henry was to howl hound-dog style and to run around the farm lifting his leg on every tire on tractors, trucks, and cars. We had to constantly hose down the tires to prevent damage to all the vehicles.

Scooter could be heard hunting anything that came on the farm. I found him running around a tree where he held a cat captive, maybe from the next farm, by howling at the top of his lungs. This was way out of anything I had experienced with dogs. I went up to Scooter and looked him straight on and yelled that he should stop. To my surprise, he stopped and went back to the barn. The cat then came out of the tree and went home. Amazingly, Scooter continued to hunt anything that came on the farm but silently. He and Henry still did their howling bouts anytime a siren passed our highway. I kept thinking Danes don't howl but they do if someone teaches them.

Henry was a typical young dog and loved to chew on interesting items. Most of the time he wasn't too destructive because things could be replaced. There was an incident, however, when Ernie, in preparation for work, had all of his belongings arranged on the bed so as not to forget anything. He prepared to leave to teach an aviation class and looked for his wallet. He knew it had laid out with all of the other items he needed, including the wallet. We searched the house for hours with no success. What could have happened to the wallet? The mystery was solved when we noticed that Henry's mouth seemed to have something protruding from the sides. Upon closer inspection, Henry had the wallet and had been walking around in front of us for over an hour.

The next thing we discovered was that no matter how good our five-foot horse fencing was, Scooter got around it. Then Henry decided he should go on these adventures too. One day I looked to our far field across the canal to see what looked like a deer bounding through the tall grass. Suddenly I realized it was Henry, and there was another animal trailing along behind him. I ran over and Henry came right away. I couldn't figure out how Henry had gotten over the fence. Scooter was a lost cause and I had to just let him do his own thing, but Henry wasn't so street smart, so I kept really good tabs on him. Scooter didn't want anything to do with the house, thank heavens, because he loved to find the nastiest things to roll in. It was a blessing that Henry didn't learn that!

When I let Henry out during the evenings, I put a collar on him that had a light. His gray merle color helped him disappear in the dark. One evening as I checked on Henry doing his nightly business, I saw what appeared to be a light on the other side of the fence. It was slightly obscured by a row of apple trees, so as I walked along trying to find this light, it suddenly leaped into the air and landed in front of me. Henry had just leaped over a five-foot fence in one bound from a total stop. The mystery of how Henry went on the Scooter romps was now clear.

Henry had fun every day following the mischievous Scooter. Even though Scooter had been neutered, he was always seeking greener pastures; thirty-three acres wasn't enough. He was smart enough to understand that he was to stay on this side of the farm. It was the difference between the outdoor Scooter and the indoor, soft, sensitive Henry, and why Scooter became the best hunter for a friend's farm.

Cats were safe with Henry. Once when he was walking around the yard, we noticed he had something hanging from his mouth. We knew he liked to carry items around and was always willing to show you what he had. This time when we opened his mouth, there was a tiny face looking at us. He had found one of the kittens that a stray cat living in the barn had tucked into the haystacks. He certainly was a gentle giant, and the kitten was perfectly okay and taken back to the mother. We think the kitten had wandered away and Henry decided to protect it. It was amazing how he carried the kitten around without harming it. What we had noticed was the tail hanging out of Henry's mouth.

Henry was friendly and best friends with a doll-faced Persian cat who lounged with Henry on the L-shaped couch. He truly loved not only horses but cats as well. Later, there were two additional cats that were adopted when several stray kittens appeared among the haystacks, having been abandoned.

I came to grips with the fact that each dog breed has definite characteristics. This is why I came to love Danes: they loved horses and are good inside the house. Henry would never think of rolling in the neighbor's cow dung. This realization of definite breed characteristics also came to pass when a horse helper asked if she could bring her Australian collie to run around to get rid of his energy.

We carefully introduced everyone, and it seemed all right. Henry was very much the follower and not at all a barker or aggressive. What happened was an eye opener. We were standing outside one of the horse stalls with the dogs gathered next to the stall where the horse had his head out looking at all of us. All of the Danes have been easy and friendly with the horses, often going into their stalls to get a horse backrub. So, Henry was very friendly with Foxie, a Russian Orlov Rostopchin—they were friends. What happened next amazed and shocked us all. It was difficult to see what happened first, but the new Aussie visitor probably took exception to Henry standing next to all of the adults and the horse. Our visiting dog suddenly barked and we all recognized it was serious when he began to attack Henry in an instant. The owner tried to no avail to take her dog from Henry. Henry did nothing to protect himself or his long legs as he followed me while I half-carried him, trying to keep him away from the biting dog. The short distance to the house seemed miles while the frantic owner used all of her weight to try and pin her dog down. His strength was incredible for his size. Henry dutifully followed me, allowing me to half-carry him, and we finally made it safely to the door of the house. Both my friend and I were in shock as we realized our arms and hands were inches from the biting dog, now sitting calmly as if nothing had happened.

Henry had bites all up and down his legs and it took our vet quite some time to treat them all. We couldn't figure out what had precipitated this attack since everything was going so well. It was then I decided to talk this over with my farrier. We had a suspicion of what started it all, but with both of our hands right where Henry was being bitten, how did we avoid injury? He described that these dogs were raised to protect sheep from predators and Henry triggered this protective reaction. The reason we weren't bitten was these dogs are so focused on what they consider the predator that the bites were totally directed at Henry. Interestingly, water was hosed on the offending dog by the third person who had the presence of mind to try this. It had no effect. My farrier, who has many years of experience working in some stressful, difficult situations, suggested that using a lead line tightly around the neck of the attacking dog might have given us less time with Henry being bitten, but he added that the dog might have turned his attention on the person now preventing him from getting Henry.

My friend who loves animals was shaken that this family pet suddenly was unrecognizable. She came every day to help with the horses. We often talked about what happened while we cleaned stalls to try and figure out what we could have done. Remorse is a relentless creature and we both kept thinking about what we could have foreseen that would have prevented the situation.

Henry recovered from all the bites and continued to be an easy-going Dane. It was noticeable that Scooter was in charge, Henry being the younger, more submissive one. We carefully supervised Scooter and Henry to ensure that Scooter's dominant personality didn't influence Henry too much, and especially since Scooter was protective of his catches. Since Scooter spent most of his time hunting all the unseen animals that came onto the farm and Henry had no interest, we observed that there would be little conflict. We were now all the wiser and paid careful attention to these behaviors. During this time, we had few rodents and other troublesome interlopers. At one point before getting Scooter, the rats were so bad that when I fed the horses, they would be lined up on the feed bowl edge waiting for me to dump the food in. They showed no fear from me or the horses. They would jump into the feed bowl and Star, the Trakehner stallion, willingly shared his food. This wasn't a healthy situation, so Scooter had earned his keep by eliminating the unwelcome guests, and his talents were soon used on our friend's farm when Scooter became their new helper, and there was no need for dangerous poisons.

Because I knew each horse breed has particular characteristics and is bred for those such as eventing, dressage, cross-country, and Western, all the horses were suitable for specific interests. Each dog breed also has their own unique specialties; we had learned an important lesson. It's so easy to ignore that each animal has their own specific characteristics. It was a reminder, remembering the Jack Russel dogs doing their work in the chicken barn; Irma had no interest in rats just like Henry had no interest in Scooter's animal captures. My friend's dog was only doing what his breeding had programed him to perform—to protect the herd.

Sometime after this incident Henry developed bone cancer in his front leg where he was injured. Again, Dr. Thomas helped us thoughtfully think through the possible solutions for a tall, active Great Dane. Sadly, after using a leg brace as much as someone with an almost broken leg, and negatively progressing, my horse vet Dr. Best thankfully came to send Henry peacefully to the rainbow bridge.

Henry's Story

There was hardly anything to remember about my beginning except I suddenly found myself alone in a room. I was taken to a place where I was transferred to a car and then another room. There were more people in the room and a kind lady who paid attention to me and tried to make me feel at home as I sat by the door. She took me over to a couch and allowed me to sit on it. It was the most comfortable place I had ever been.

Even though I was an outstanding example of my type, there wasn't a great deal of care given to me, and I was especially thin.

Several days passed and I was being fed regularly and had a comfortable place to sleep. I was sitting quietly on the couch when my mistress became worried that I didn't seem quite right. I was a quiet personality, but she thought there was something not right. She took my temperature. It was right after Christmas and so the regular vet wasn't available. She immediately took me to an emergency clinic, and luckily it was caught in time, and they did surgery to save my life. She took me home the next day and I happily felt much better.

Being an easy-going personality, I was easy to train. I had total freedom and thought the long-legged animals were friendly. Everything went along perfectly for a long time, when one day another dog arrived. He was much shorter and was rather undignified. He loved to roll in dirt and smelled horrible, so it was good he didn't come in the house. He loved to hunt all kinds of animals. He was kind of unpleasant and as much as I enjoyed following him around, I was happier with my family. He finally left.

One day another dog came to visit and seemed friendly. My horse friend and I were sharing rubs when suddenly this visitor attacked me. My mistress immediately stepped in to protect me. This was shocking because this thing was half my size, so he bit my leg. I didn't know what to do but my mistress half-carried me to the safety of the house. She started to clean my legs and then put me in the car. I was nervous but I trusted her.

Soon we were at my favorite vet, and they started to fix my legs. They gave me medicine and my mistress took me home to the comfort of my bed. Pretty soon all the bites healed, and I was back to running around.

The farm was a wonderful place, and I was always free to visit my friend Foxie. Life continued with runs until one day my mistress saw I didn't make a full movement with my front leg; it didn't seem right. She was accustomed to always checking her horses. It didn't seem serious, but she took me to our vet. They X-rayed my leg and the news wasn't good; I could tell because she seemed worried. It was the beginning of a serious problem, so I wore a thing on my leg that helped me walk with less pain. She kept taking me to the vet until there was nothing more to be done.

Alexandria Allie – Puppy Eyes

For over a year I filled out all the paperwork to rescue a Great Dane, and to the chagrin of my two vets who wrote copious letters having known me for over fifteen years, we were refused. After we had unsuccessfully tried to rescue a Great Dane for over a year it was all because they said we had horses.

Thinking about coincidence, I suddenly decided to look for a Great Dane on the internet with really no intent of finding my next companion. I found a picture of the cutest black Great Dane with puppy eyes. Often, we make emotional decisions. There was the sudden connection with a black Great Dane that looked just like the beautiful black Spanish Great Dane Tiki and the German Irma. Her puppy picture brought back a flood of wonderful memories. The breeder was later discovered to personally manage her Danes in the way I treat my horses. She became a wonderful resource of Alexandria's beginning, and we communicated often, sharing pictures. It was wonderful to have insight into the background of my Great Dane, with a wonderful home beginning that became a glaring contrast to a future Great Dane. Now in hindsight, I am sure that the first experiences a puppy has will create a strong memory. When I opened the shipping crate, Alexandria acted as if she knew me; there wasn't any apprehension as I picked her up.

I received the following introduction:

> Hello! My name is Alexandria! Of course you can call me whatever you like, but my first mom called me this and followed by "c'mere"…I usually came. When she was giving me a treat and I go too excited, she would hold it up and tell me "You know what you have to do to get this!"(personal communication from first mom)

This letter closed with the request to share occasional photos and communicate. It was the beginning of not only having a beautiful Great Dane but getting to know more than I ever was able to know about any of my previous Great Danes. It made the experience with Allie more personal as I continually sent photos and shared Allie stories. These Allie stories sent by email became the idea for inclusion in my horse books and finally this story about Great Danes,

Alexandria became Allie for short because this was an easy command to teach her, which she learned quickly. This was true because of her caring start that she was easily trained, It was important on the farm that she would come immediately when called. Her training was successful as illustrated in the following story. She was wonderful with the horses and two of the horses became her favorites: Foxie the Russian and the mare Firebird the Hungarian. She would stand outside Foxie's stall getting her back scratched. Firebird would always share her meals, so when I fed the mare, Allie was always assured of a free meal as she scooped up the grain that escaped.

The excellent book, *The Great Dane Puppy Handbook: A Complete Guide to the First Year* (2020), provided interesting ideas about some important first-year concepts. I am always researching ideas about horses and

Great Danes. Since Allie was the first Dane purchased from a breeder through the internet, the book has compelling thoughts about several ways to assure acquiring a healthy Great Dane. I was fortunate with my decision as the book describes the importance of contact with the breeder. They cheerfully contacted me as soon as I made the purchase. This continued when they sent pictures of Allie, and I continually relayed the cute stories about her life here on the farm. It was wonderful to get to know about Allie's past.

Since I had a home office for my counseling work, Allie was always with me. Allie became a center for always feeling secure even when I was alone on the farm. She was always calm and never showed any aggressiveness. I could pull into a gas station with her sitting in her safely netted second-row seat and she would never bark if anyone came near the car. People often would ask if they could pet her, and she loved the attention. The airline-designed net that would protect her from being tossed even over the high seat assured that she was comfortable, stretched out, and safe in the event of a sudden stop.

Allie's peaceful attitude continued when we had an experience that changed my understanding of how astute Allie analyzed everyone she met. We parked, drinking coffee at a McDonald's restaurant. I had the driver's side window open when a panhandler came up to the window and reached in, attempting to get money. The high seats hid the lounging Great Dane seated in her second-row place. Unknown to the hand reaching in was how close he was to danger. Suddenly, Allie revealed her protective nature with a surprisingly distinctive, aggressive, deep loud growl that we had never heard.

The chap leaped back, noticing that a large black figure was seated behind me. This was an eye opener to realize that Allie knew exactly who to distrust. She never had greeted anyone with even a bark. She often sat quietly when the back of the SUV was loaded with sacks of horse food, and she looked over the seat until she was finally noticed. People were often surprised and amazed how unusually calm she was, atypical for a dog in a car.

Because of what had happened with Henry being bitten by what we thought was a family dog, I was overly protective of Allie. She did have one trustworthy friend named Happy. This cute, lovable lapdog was the companion of my farrier Steve and his wife Sharon, who often visited the farm. Allie was so careful when she played with the little Shih Tzu that it was fun to watch. Allie was huge compared to Happy, but they ran around in the yard playing, with Allie crouching down and never using her paws or barking. Happy, however, barked at Allie, attempting to get her to play and run around. Allie and Happy were play buddies and I never had to worry about Allie getting her legs bitten.

We did have a close call with a neighbor's Australian Collie when he found a way around the fence between the farms. During one of our excursions around the farm, the dog suddenly appeared and was running toward us. Immediately my thoughts went to what happened with Tiki on the beach, and to Henry. Allie was acting friendly because she didn't have any experience with an unfriendly dog. She was wagging her tail, so I knew that she was unaware of the danger. The dog kept acting aggressively, coming at us, and it started lunging at Allie. Allie still didn't understand so I grabbed a horse blanket that was on the ATV and began swinging it at the attacking dog. He ran off, back in the direction of his farm, as the owner ran across the field trying to get his dog. Allie and I turned and went as quickly as possible and ran to the safety of the main farm. I drove the ATV as fast as I could, and Allie was ahead, leading us back home.

After this incident I kept a heavy walking stick on the ATV. They apparently fixed the fence where the dog escaped because each time we did our farm excursions, the dog was only running up and down safely on the other side of the fence. It became a safe game and Allie would engage with the dog, running on her side of the fence. We would do our trip each day to check the farm. Allie would look to see if her "friend" was there to play the fence running game. The dog would hide behind a bush near the fence until we approached and then the game would begin. One trip Allie looked for the dog to play the game but the dog wasn't there. Each day, Allie looked for the dog to play the game. She did this for many trips. She didn't know what I knew; that the farm had been sold to new owners and they only had horses.

We took a trip to the nearby Mount Rainer during the fall when there weren't many tourists. We drove over to a quiet picnic area that was near the living quarters of summer staff, now vacant. There wasn't a person around; we had the area to ourselves, so we let Allie free to explore. As we sat on the benches, she circled the area checking everything. It was always fun to take her to a place where there were new smells. As always she would walk within sight of us and return each time to check in. It was fun watching her as she carefully explored the surroundings, never getting out of our sight.

The afternoon was uneventful until a pair of hikers walked down the road. I called Allie and she immediately came and quietly sat next to me. The couple continued along the dirt road until they noticed Allie. What happened next surprised us because instead of waving hello, they began to bark loudly at Allie. Allie, being the more mature, merely sat quietly next to me looking at these silly people as they continued down the path. In all, the many times I had Allie on excursions she was always so quiet when meeting new people. There were only two exceptions: the duck hunter and the panhandler.

Almost every day we would take a ride with the ATV with Allie running along as we made the trip around the edge of the farm. We had systematically worked to athletically progress so she was able to run over twenty-five miles an hour and faster than I could drive. She would run ahead and then wait for me to catch up. Our vet noticed how physically fit she was. I had to check the farm, especially during duck season, because of poachers. Part of the farm had wetland during several months, so ducks and geese thought it a nice place to hang out. Allie thought this was fun and as soon as I started up the ATV, she was ready for the outing and happily ran to the beginning of our path.

The sea son progressed with more and more water on the back fields. Allie became accustomed to running over the now water-covered fields. I had to watch where I drove the ATV and stayed along a path that ran along the canal, but Allie thought this was great fun as she sailed over places I couldn't go with the ATV. We didn't realize that we were training for a big event. Thinking back about our daily adventures, it shouldn't have been a surprise because Allie had been practicing her wetland skills.

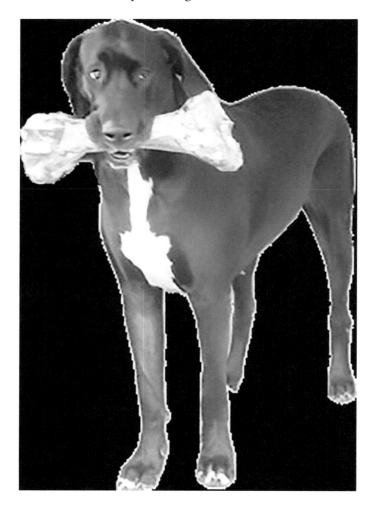

One of Allie's favorite trips was to go shopping with me because she knew I would buy her a huge bone. She was also a connoisseur of coffee and half and half. If a cup were left on the table, it would be found perfectly standing but a little missing. It is not good for dogs to have caffeine and after we realized her love for coffee with mostly half and half, we tried to keep them out of her reach. This is definitely on the list of shouldn't eat for dogs. The reason we discovered her fetish was that near the cup, the tablecloth was damp. The mystery was discovered when finally, Allie was seen carefully drinking a cup of coffee. Otherwise, she never took anything off the table or touched food. It was amazing how careful and dainty she drank her coffee *au lait*. She was lady-like even at her birthday party when she patiently waited to be told she could eat the cake sitting in front of her. Then she carefully ate her cake without making any untidiness.

While doing research for this book about Great Danes, the book *The Great Dane Puppy Book* has unique facts about this breed and described several interesting facts. The author also has a fun website: "15 Things I Didn't Know Until I Owned a Great Dane!" (Reed, 2020). Reading the list, it was fun to see all the things I had come to know by owning a Great Dane. One fact describing the funny Dane behavior was their aversion to rain. Allie was unflappable running over the wetland fields but when it rained, and she had to go out for potty, she would stand on the porch looking out furtively not wanting to go out in the rain. She finally figured out she could quickly run to the barn and not have to go potty in the rain. It worked perfectly for both of us because she established a place on the fallen hay on the floor in a corner of the barn. It made it easy to scoop it up and she habitually made this possible, so we had a clean yard because of her tidiness.

In her whole life she never made a mistake in the house until a horse/dog sitter failed to let her out at the appointed time, in fact the sitter never came. Since I had the door locked, she couldn't do her normal tapping the French-style flipper handle to let herself out. When I arrived home, she was sitting distressed by the door next to her accident. I could see how upset she was and let her out immediately. I told her how sorry I was for what happened and pet her so she would understand. I was so upset about this sitter. This was one of the few times when my normal helper couldn't be there and this person assured me they could do the simple job of letting Allie out and giving the horses hay. The horses were okay because they had automatic water and I had left plenty of hay.

Great Danes and horses have several things in common. The horses on the farm are all large warmbloods and easy-going. When leading them around on lines it's important that they have the security of the handler's direction. The safest position is close at their shoulder and to confidently direct them where you want them to walk. Mostly they feel assured by the confident handler who quietly directs. The reason is, there is no way to drag a 1,700-pound horse around and most trainers understand this fact when handling horses larger than a tiny mini. Great Danes also have some of these characteristics in that a handler might have a problem dragging a 180-pound dog compared to ten-pound Shih Tzu in a potentially stressful situation. Normally by walking closely and quietly directing, the handler will experience less resistance. Allie, for the most part, was easy to handle. The few times she was uncertain, merely holding her collar and keeping her close to me would get her to go where I wanted.

Allie was always well-behaved visiting the veterinary office, and her favorite vet Dr. Thomas, never had any difficulties. She would be a little reluctant to enter the door but using my close collar hold and urging her produced no problem. We quietly sat on a bench in the office waiting our turn. She was friendly to the dog sitting next to us and quietly greeted the new friend to the surprise of the owner, who wondered how such a big dog was so well-behaved. Allie sat Dane-style next to me, partially in my lap. We sat there quietly until a vet technician came to us and wanted to weigh her. She proceeded to take Allie's leash and proceeded to take her to the other side of the room where there was an ominous black mat by the wall. Allie went fine until she was forced to sit on the black mat. Next thing, Allie was running across the room dragging a surprised vet tech behind on a blue leash. Allie promptly, defiantly sat herself on my lap in the protection of her mommy.

It was time for Allie's appointment with Dr. Thomas, so we went together to the examining room, and I explained Allie was afraid of the weighing mat. She explained that it wasn't a problem and that she would weigh her when she took her to the back treatment room to give her the shots. Allie was easily weighed.

The full story was included in my horse training book, because the positive methods used with horses are easily applied to dogs. To summarize, Allie had to be kept safe so she could freely go on excursions on the thirty-three acres that included a deep, narrow canal with steep sides. It might be dangerous to slip into, therefore I always had a long cotton rope on the ATV, just in case. She had to immediately come on the command "Allie-Allie." The story is interesting about how we slowly conditioned the six-month-old Allie to slowly walk along with an ATV, and to finally run. She soon ran faster than I could safely drive the ATV but came anytime I yelled, "Allie-Allie!" This was wonderful as Allie loved running in the fields that often became wetland. The story continued until the two-and-a-half-year-old Allie weighed 180 pounds and could run over twenty-five miles an hour over any surface, including the wetland that ran along the path.

The story occurred in late January at sunset:

Allie and I are finishing our run and have stopped along the canal to enjoy the scenery on the other side. It has turned dark, and the moon is beautifully reflected on the wetland field. We are heading back on the dry side of the canal. Allie is sitting right next to me when I see she is intently staring across the canal to the far trees next to the shining wetland field. She sees something, and I strain to see what Allie is staring at in the far distance when an ominous, dark-cloaked figure suddenly appears at the edge of the distant trees. The lumbering figure starts splashing, wading through the wet field carrying a huge sack. The figure is totally unaware he's being watched, being tracked, by a huge dog that is larger than a male black panther.

The rest of this story unfolds in split seconds. Allie in her time with us hardly barks more than a one-bark notice and has never shown any aggressive behavior. I could hardly believe what happened next. I realize this dark figure is a duck poacher who is setting decoys for an early morning hunt poaching on our property. As I yell, "Get off our property!" I realize that Allie is barking furiously, growling, and to my horror is airborne, soaring over the canal. I anticipate pulling her out of the canal, but my fears are allayed as I see her running, hardly touching the water, and closing now within seconds of the dark, retreating figure, who realizes he is being chased and frantically is trying to reach the barbwire fence that he cut. Allie has covered what would be a deep-water-covered football field in seconds. She is within several yards from the poacher when I realize

I cannot let her take this figure down for several reasons—mostly her safety. She is going to defend me at all cost; I can hear it in her continued angry barking as she pursues this fiend. This frantically stumbling, cumbersomely dressed poacher knows this isn't a miniature birddog chasing him and probably can't imagine what animal can run across nearly ten inches of water that fast. At the top of my lungs I yell the cue, "Allie-Allie!" In midair, Allie turns and starts running back to me as I stay put and keep calling to her. When suddenly out of the darkness she flies back across the canal and is sitting next to me, looking expectantly with her cute, soft, puppy-like eyes as if to say, "Well, where's my treat?" I exhale and reach into my pocket and hand her a treat. Everything is as it was—a beautiful, quiet evening, with a splendid moon shining over the wetland (Dammier, 2019, p.123).

Even though we may not recognize them, there are strong bonds that we have created with both horses and dogs, which have become just as strong as the behavior we teach them. This is called our relationship, created by all the positive times of being together.

One of the items on the "15 Things I Didn't Know Until I Owned a Great Dane" was following the owner into the bathroom. With Allie, she only followed me when she figured out I was getting ready to leave by doing extra hair and makeup. She would come and sit, watching me to make sure I wouldn't forget to take her. Most of the time I did take her unless she might have to wait too long in the car. Life for Allie was wonderful, and she was always with me.

Anytime I had to go someplace alone I took Allie with me, especially to Seattle. I never would have picked the unsafe Seattle but this doctor specialized in stem cell procedures that were helping with my overtaxed joints from the horse activities. This clinic was the nearest specialist I had discovered from my research. Besides handling the horses and Great Danes, I needed to continue the support for the farm; other options would have made me give everything up. So, Allie was my protection on this trip alone, because she is much more efficient than a concealed permit. His office and protected parking lot are safe but surrounding this area there are very unsavory characters. The worry is when stopping for a light that they approach the cars—extremely unnerving! I knew I would be safe with Allie's protection.

Shortly after what seemed a normal routine, Allie didn't quite seem herself with no real symptoms after checking her vitals. Because of having had horses for many years, I am accustomed to paying attention anytime they seem different, so I immediately took Allie to her favorite vet. Dr. Thomas who gave her a thorough exam as Allie sat half on my lap and she felt her abdomen. The X-rays, which included her lungs, explained why she didn't seem like herself. She had completed all of her shots and blood work only four months ago. Her sudden sickness left us shocked. Dr. Thomas sadly noted that Allie was totally physically fit in every way except for the serious cancer rapidly overwhelming her body. A few days later, the X-rays that were sent to a specialist confirmed the terminal cancer. Even though Allie appeared much like herself, there was an ominous threat of a sudden collapse while walking around. Again, I turned to Dr. Thomas to think through the necessary decision and my horse vet Dr. Daily to help Allie's peaceful transition.

During a lifetime of horses and Great Danes, I have had to make tough decisions; they've all been difficult, and I steeled my way through the process each time. This time it was later that the stark contrast of not having Allie with me hit me, and I was suddenly faced with an intense feeling of loss…I had to try and replace her.

*As of this writing a new blood test for a,, cancer diagnosis has been announced. (https://www.AKC.org)

Allie's Story

Being the family of eight, I had a wonderful start with constant attention because I had a family to take care of me. I was a beautiful black color with a perfect white bib. My family showed my mother and because we were so lovely we were advertised by an agency that provided publicity for people who were serious about having a Great Dane. A lady who sadly had lost her companion found my picture on the internet and fell in love with me because long ago she had a dear friend who looked like me.

The arrangement was made and shortly a kind face opened my shipping crate and carefully set me on a grassy spot so I could finally relieve myself. She carefully set me safely on the long seat behind her and we were off. I felt as if I knew her, and everything would be the same. And it was. I had my own couch and was free to walk around except for the kitchen, and the back hallway. Later I was allowed to go everywhere, even sit on her bed. A grassy place near a tree outside the house became my first potty place—I learned this in four days! I followed her around as she helped me learn my way around the farmyard; I always stayed in this area until she began to teach me to follow her. She taught me to always come when she called "Allie-Allie." As I grew stronger, she slowly increased our exercise.

I was definitely a mommy's dog because we were always together. There was never lots of leash training because what was important was that I always came when called, so I really didn't need a leash. I was friendly with everyone, and I could tell the few times there were bad people and alerted her. If I were free, I would immediately come and stay with her. She took me everywhere with her and I would sit quietly with my large bone. I was always quiet and never barked if anyone came near the car because I knew the difference between who was dangerous and who was just walking around.

Everyday there were new things. The long-legged animals were friends. Two of them became my favorites, especially the dark brown one who shared her food. Now that I came every time she called, she took me on longer runs. I would run a short distance and she would slow so I would walk. This was great fun. There were wonderful smells from all the animals that lived in the field. My days were filled with fun things to do: visits to friends, sleeping on my couch, sitting with mommy while she sat at her desk, and going for rides in the car. The best thing was to come when I began to learn to follow her when she had to patrol the back of the farm. There were strangers coming on the farm; I could smell them.

I had a small friend who came to visit. Happy, as she was well-named, was so tiny that I was careful when we played. Her friends didn't worry about me playing with their small doggie. My other friend was fun to play with as long as he was on the other side of the farm properties, and we would chase each other along the fence to see which one of us was faster. One time he was on our property, and I thought he came running to me while we were going around the farm. I thought this would be fun to play but my mommy was smarter and knew this was trouble. He immediately began snapping at my long legs and she went into action. I still didn't understand what was happening. She called me and I at once went to her. It was surprising but she grabbed a large blanket off the ATV and started swinging it, and the dog ran off to his owner, who now knew his dog had escaped and had come to get him. She called me and we ran home immediately. After that he stayed on his side of the fence. It was fun to do the fence run as long as he couldn't bite my legs. She was very protective of me. It was as if she knew something I didn't understand.

One cool evening before sunset after we finished our patrol, we were next to the canal, and I was sitting attentively by her side. She didn't see what I first saw in the distance. When she focused on what I was staring at, she yelled at this stranger. I knew right away this lumbering figure was up to mischief. Leaping in the air, I flew over the canal and began the chase to get this monster off my property. I was at my peak running speed and leaped across the wetland in seconds. For over a year I had been practicing and loved to run in the fields covered with water. Afterall, I was almost three feet tall at my shoulders. This water was hardly anything to me. I was almost ready to grab this thing when my mistress yelled my special call and I obediently turned back to her, even though I wanted to get this thing. I quickly ran back in case she needed me. In a second I was flying over the canal and sitting by her side. She looked down, stroked my head, and gave me one of my favorite treats. It was now dark, and the light came from overhead. I sensed that she was calm, and we slowly returned home. I did a good job; I protected her.

Several years later my visits to the back fields where I loved to go were at a slower pace, because she could see I didn't have the energy that I used to have. After all, I was now almost eight years old, which is getting old for a Great Dane. She would stop in our favorite place so I could walk around checking the new scents. Every field visit I would check the beaver hut they had built at the edge of the canal. They were happy to own their own place where nobody chased them. I spent more time on my couch sleeping while keeping an eye out for what she was doing.

My last duty before I became seriously ill was to protect her when she had to drive alone to an unsafe place. Every time I went with her, I could smell that there were unpleasant people around. The place where we parked was quiet with nobody around but going to this place, I could tell there were threatening people who would approach the car when we stopped. I made sure that they knew I was there in the back seat.

Besides the coffee I snitched, there were wonderful meals with vegetables and freshly cooked chicken or hamburger, and specially baked cakes with lighted sticks on them. Happily, life had continued until one day I went to visit my favorite vet. It was hard to breathe, and I was feeling tired. We went to visit the vet several times, but it was getting harder for me. I could tell that my mistress was worried about me because she sat next to me while I was sleeping. We visited my favorite vet several more times. One time she stood next to the car where I was quietly sitting, and they talked for a long time. It didn't sound like the way they used to talk. I was trying to continue doing everything normally, but I felt very tired. Finally, she found a way for me to go to sleep on my own couch. Someone who I didn't know was with her as she sat next to me looking differently than I had ever seen her. I looked at her with my puppy eyes so she'd know I was all right. She quietly stroked my head until I finally closed my eyes for the last time—I felt her love.

Charlotte

There have been numerous times when I have waited to hear about one of my four-legged family members being shipped. Several times I have been involved with the shipment of flying two of my horses from Germany to Los Angeles when I handled all the paperwork and delivering them to the Frankfurt airport and getting them on the plane to accompany them to Los Angeles. This was certainly a nail-biter being at a distance and hoping to get the necessary information.

It only seems like yesterday that I waited for a shipment to the Alaska Airlines Cargo Center in Seattle. I wondered if I could be so lucky again to have everything go as scheduled, pick up a crate, and see a happy Great Dane puppy. It was only eight years ago that I had picked up my beloved Allie, only to find myself doing the same thing again. I prayed it would all go as well.

Because it's been eight years since I picked up a shipment, I missed the turn since the building has been updated with a new look. Turning around, I found the parking lot that was now lined with waiting vehicles in front of the building. As I was standing in line, a woman came out to ask if anyone was waiting for a young puppy. I immediately indicated my presence. She smilingly said that was good and brought Charlotte's crate from her office. Alaska was so efficient that Charlotte made it over to the office forty-five minutes after the plane landed. We had tracked the flight on the internet—as a pilot I'm interested in viewing the flight data—so we knew exactly when she landed. The moment of anticipation had arrived and as we opened the crate, an apprehensive face greeted us. We petted her and lifted her out of the shipping container. At first, she was worried about getting into the car until she sniffed the seat where Allie always sat. She then promptly allowed us to place her in the safe long seat with the safety net. We were off to her new home.

Charlotte has a fantastic pedigree, and the breeder successfully breeds Great Danes worth much as show dogs. This, however, is not the reason I again went to the internet to try and find a companion to replace the loss of Allie. Charlotte is a beautiful example of a Great Dane, fortunately not only is she as lovely as Allie with a shiny black coat and partially white bib, but underneath her lack of quiet adult handling is a wonderfully kind, sweet, and loving dog. She has responded to becoming part of a home although we jokingly call her Miss Piggy because of her deportment, especially after she jumped into the dirty little runoff near the barn.

The farm has a small space the size of a kiddie pool that collects water runoff from the building and is a rather dirty mixture. We observed her on one of her first days with supervised freedom running across the courtyard with a huge leap, launching herself into the muddy water and joyously rolling around! Heavens, was our highly bred dog another Scooter? We think our American Kennel Club (AKC) bred Great Dane had enough of the high-class kennel life and wanted to enjoy being a farm dog. She promptly received a bath to restore her original Great Dane dignity.

My perhaps trivial decision and worry about picking a pet by its sweet face and breeding was quickly allayed and I am so happy to have Charlotte as part of our family. It is obvious that Charlotte was carefully raised, but in a kennel situation. Breeders take much effort to give these energetic puppies the attention they need, and it makes a difference, but the people handling the puppies don't always understand playing overly energetically with a young puppy begins habits at a young learning point.

The excellent book about the first year of a Great Dane puppy had many insights that I had researched but rethought as I approached a new puppy that was noticeably different than the easy-going Allie. It was difficult to not compare the two Great Danes. One of the important facts mentioned by Reed (2020), is that upon the sale, the breeder should be available to talk to the new owner. I tried through the intermediary and by sending a personal letter to contact the breeder, with unfortunately no results. They probably will never see the wonderful life that their beautiful puppy is enjoying, or do they care? I have received a gorgeous puppy who is turning out perfectly thanks to my patience and positive training knowledge. I don't really need any more information from the breeder because I have observed her behavior and what she reacts to.

We soon discovered that there must have been a crew of young folks taking care of the puppies, especially a young helper of about twenty that must have taken care of Charlotte. We had a young driver with a delivery for the farm who alerted us to her attachment to any young person. When he stepped out of the truck, he was worried about her size until she went crazy wagging her tail and trying to roughly play with him. He noticed how happy she was, especially when she tried to get into the truck with him.

Charlotte was originally given the nickname Cookie, but we changed it to Sharlie because when called outside it would carry over a distance. When she saw my young horse helper, Heather, she became frantically excited, acting as if she knew her. This was at a distance of a hundred feet. Later, Sharlie tried to follow Heather when she got into her car. Every time Heather comes to help with the horses, Sharlie becomes excited and tries to see her. She acts as if she has known Heather forever. It was amazing to all of us but obviously at this Great Dane breeding establishment there were young caretakers who took care of Charlotte as a puppy. It's wonderful that there were young people to care for the puppies and they certainly were handled in a fun way because she was an outgoing, exuberant pup. This was going to be a challenge of beginning an adult atmosphere with controlled play.

We were soon to discover many differences in the way Allie and Charlotte were raised, because the differences were imbedded in their behavior. We have a problem that is to be solved. There is an important part when animals are young to create habits, so while she is pleasant with people and other animals, she gets out of control because she sees young folks as aggressive playtime, trying to grab things and jumping. This has already changed because when Heather comes to help with the horses, Charlotte has learned to sit quietly and get a treat.

When a pet owner loses a beloved pet the only thing that seems to fill in the loss is another pet to love. Even though I have rescued several dogs, it was important to have the Great Dane characteristics that I discovered with Irma, my first Dane. All you're looking for is all those wonderful moments that are missing, and to replace the emptiness without them.

The thoughts from the book *A Dog's Purpose* (2010) states it so perfectly: Laugh, love, and save someone. Truly it is an act of reciprocation—giving in return. Sharlie has already started to make us laugh again at her silly puppy antics and saved us from missing Allie. And so, the new journey begins, but it is going to take all our energy to get Sharlie to become steady. The positive part is that she gets to run in the protective confines of the farm; never to be kenneled. Run? Boy does she ever! She has discovered her legs and the fun of running around the high-fenced farm courtyard. It is so typical of each of the Great Danes of this story as they each discovered the freedom to run.

When the farm property was purchased, it was on a sleepy road that hardly had any traffic. Slowly the area has built up and the road outside the farm has become a main thoroughfare, making it important to have good fencing and a high-tech gate so we wouldn't have to worry about horses or dogs getting out on the now-busily traveled road. Even with the best precautions, unfortunate events happen. In my book about the horses, I tell stories about coincidences. The chances of all those things happening at the same time are impossible to explain. Of course, part of the explanation is that if they didn't occur, a tragedy is most likely the outcome.

In the last several weeks Sharlie has learned to safely explore the surroundings of the house and barns, and hasn't sought to press the fencing as many dogs are likely to do at great peril. A watchful eye was kept on Sharlie as she happily accompanied me doing farm chores. She stayed close until during some farm work with a smaller tractor triggered the automatic gate to open and the curious Sharlie found herself in seconds on the outside, with no one aware of what unexpectedly happened. No one except for Nikki, one of our talented dressage riders, who just happened to drive by as Sharlie appeared in the driveway by the road. Nikki brought her to the safety of the farm. Nikki couldn't have been in this exact place in a million years, but she just happened to be driving by the farm right at the moment to keep Sharlie safe. Nikki rode and competed with several of the German dressage horses when they were younger, before life moved everyone on, and many of the horses retired. She thought at first it was Allie and then realized it looked similar to an Allie puppy.

In this serious occurrence, coincidence seemed to play a role in another miraculous conclusion. As a psychologist and a researcher, I was drawn to review what was written on the subject. Most of the original work in this field was done by the famous psychologist Jung. The psychologist Beitman, in his book *Meaningful Coincidences* (2022), extends the research. He describes these experiences in interesting terms of how surprising the coincidence becomes will signify how much attention it demands from us. This incident certainly captured my attention when I thought that Sharlie was spared a possible accident by the singular chance occurrence of a friend who lives on the other side of the main nearby town. Interestingly, Beitman (2022) suggested that there is more to coincidences than randomness or fate involved in these incidences. His research posits that there may be more to synchronicities than mere luck. It really seems that there is more in these events than luck.

Sharlie had the opportunity to meet a friend's dog during their visit. Happy is the cutest little Shih Tzu that Allie had played together with on several occasions. Since Great Danes by their nature are kind and easy going, it was decided to let Happy and Sharlie meet while the adults were enjoying conversation. Sharlie was considerate of the tiny dog in comparison to her and the introduction went well until Sharlie began to jump excitedly. Even though she wasn't hurting Happy, it was too rough for the tiny Happy, who immediately climbed into her owner's lap for safety. Sharlie only needs more time to not become overexcited and she'll be a perfect friend. She is already well-behaved with the horses and respectfully stands without any antics.

There are many areas for Sharlie's training. Even though she is making excellent progress, it would be easy to resort to punitive measures to stop Sharlie's attempts to play rough games. This type of behavior has a similar result while working with young horses. Since my expertise is working with horse behavior, each one of my horses born and raised on the farm tended to play rough as youngsters. As a result, using force to stop bad behavior may result in decreased confidence and worse, invite retaliation for being struck. For many using force it is simple and seems a quick solution. Often, though, there are negative resulting consequences, such as what happened with the beautiful Harley. Both dogs and horses are quick to recognize the delayed moving hand.

Horses and dogs often become extremely aggressive as they seek to protect themselves from being struck. They become quick to recognize the human preparation to strike. There is no way that an owner wants what will be a 100-pound-plus dog to become aggressive; the remedy is almost impossible. To provide a quick explanation, if quiet behavior such as sitting or standing quietly is rewarded, inappropriate behavior such as nipping, jumping, or grabbing is decreased. In the example, we effectively used the command to sit to stop the grabbing, jumping, and playful nipping.

Honestly, at the beginning of this adventure, there was definitely doubt about how the training would progress. Even though Sharlie had a lovely character and was sweet, she was inclined to being spontaneously rough, which was worrisome. I was not sure of being successful. Since the years I spent with Allie were so easy and wonderful, there was some uncertainty to whether Sharlie would reach the same level. Again, she is sitting with me on the couch with her head on my lap. Happily, with positive consistency, she is steadily becoming a wonderful companion.

Reviewing the last several months, it seems that Sharlie needed time to become accustomed to a consistent schedule and being free in the house and on the farm. She may have been overwhelmed with the contrast of her previous situation. She has responded happily to having free run of the main part of the house with her own couch. Also, she enjoys being able to be outside in the protected courtyard and going on trips to the barn to care for the horses. The horses are happy with Great Danes and the mare especially has taken to Sharlie the way she did with Allie.

If you review the story about Harley, she was nipping at moving hands because she had been struck. We didn't want to have Sharlie lose confidence in us when it is easy to use positive commands that are rewarded to change her negative actions of thinking any hand movement cued rough play. Great Danes are sensitive, loving, wanting to please types of dogs and so this should be an asset and carefully protected. We identified the two cues that prompted the unwanted behavior: hand movements and young people. As with Harley, the hand cue now became a signal for other acceptable behaviors. With few errors, Sharlie now sits upon the waving of the hand.

There are so many things to remember about raising a puppy, especially one that is already fifty-six pounds and had to have a larger crate to fly because she was also tall. It only seems like yesterday that I was raising young horses and Danes. Where did the time go? Here I go again!

We're already starting to train Sharlie to safely follow the ATV to go on the slow, short run to the back field. She won't have to fend off duck hunters because the field is no longer interesting to ducks because it is overgrown with grass. Ducks don't like places where they can't see predators. When the fields were cut there was vast open water. This is no longer true. No water, no duck hunters.

Sharlie had a big test when one of the horses walked out of their stall while I was cleaning. In front of the stall is a large pasture, so the mare walked over to the next stall to visit her friend. When I realized that Sharlie was with me and I also had a horse free, I was concerned, but Sharlie was amazing and never barked. She quietly stood near the mare while she talked to her friend in the next stall through the opened window. Sharlie has already demonstrated being quiet walking around in the large stalls while I clean. The horses all like dogs, especially the mare. Interestingly, the mare gave Sharlie a long sniff as if she knew this was a different dog, but everything was okay. The horses are all accustomed to being touched because I wanted them to be comfortable if they were tapped on their legs or sides when taking care of them. They are totally unconcerned even when I have clumsily tapped them with the plastic rake while cleaning in their stalls.

I asked Sharlie to come with me to the gate and told her to stay there while I closed it and proceeded to get the mare back in her stall. Sharlie stayed quietly, sitting by the gate while I put the mare in her stall. She never barked, even when I had to chase the mare back into her place. I was worried that Sharlie might get excited and make things more hectic, but she was quietly sitting by the gate waiting for me to return. I had some treats in my pocket and handed her one. Thie is really an amazing event for the young Sharlie. The successful attempt to help Sharlie become a cheerful house companion instead of an out-of-control puppy is happily working effectively.

Sharlie is slowly enjoying the large hay field where many animals roam. She is learning the route and already knows the path. She is allowed to run at her own speed and leaps through the grass. It is vital for a puppy Great Dane not to over exercise, lest they overstress growing legs. The important learning is that she comes as soon as she hears, "Sharlie." It is so joyful, the beginning of a new adventure.

Charlotte – Sharlie's Story

Being born in a high-class competitive kennel isn't everything it's cracked up to be. While I'm beautiful from a long line of famous Great Danes, I didn't have a family type of beginning, but no one was ever mean to me, so I have a happy, childish personality. In fact, we had several energetic young kids who took care of us and cleaned our living place. We had a wonderful ruckus time playing when the kids came each day. They never considered that even though we were small, learning to leap about and grab things wasn't going to be much fun when we were over a hundred pounds.

It was fortunate that my future mistress saw me on the internet, and it reminded her of her last companion, whose sudden loss she grieved because no one else would have put up with my childishness. She saw underneath my silliness and sometimes disruptive behavior a sweet, loving potential that could be encouraged. She followed her feelings and didn't want me crated while putting up with my nonsense but slowly allowed more freedom with the run of the living room. She taught me to sleep on my own padded couch by sleeping alongside me for more than a week until I was comfortable, instead of putting me in a crate. It worked because the couch became my comfortable place. It was a real couch with a soft cushion. It was alongside the other couches that I was allowed to sit on too. This couch was especially mine with my own pillow.

One day I saw someone I knew. I tried to run there and see her. She was fun and we ran around together. I'm sure I know her—all I want to do is return to what I remember. This is all so strange, but I am not put in a box, and I have my own couch. Also, I am allowed to run around on my own. I found this water and jumped right into it. I have a problem because I like to potty on a smooth floor. They took me on a leash to some grass. Ick! That grass tickles me! I don't know how to potty on grass unless they take me on the leash.

After a short time, I've been free in the protected courtyard, and I found a wonderful place in the barn that smelled great. I've decided this is the place to go potty. Its smells marvelous and it doesn't tickle my butt. Somebody has been here before me.

Today is the first day I get to go with my mistress as she drives a cart and I follow along. It's different and I'm worried but it is slow, and I walk following and get a treat each time she calls my name, Sharlie. This is great because we went to a big green field. There are so many smells and it's fun to run around. It's hard to know what to smell first. She called me and I got a treat. I started to walk further but she called, and I went right away to get my treat. This was a new fun day, and we explored new places.

Today we went to the big grass field but instead of the tall grass that I had to jump through it was different. There were large squares all over and it was easier for me to run. It was fun jumping over the blocks scattered across the field. I was running along and suddenly I got this terrific smell. I turned back to find the smell and several small things jumped out of a hole. I caught one and flipped it in the air and chased it when it landed in front of me. This is really cool. There wasn't anything like this where I used to live. There are two huge animals in the air circling around above. They didn't seem interested in me and my mistress isn't paying any attention to them, so I guess it's all right. It seems that they may be hunting.

At first, I was at a loss to understand how to behave. All of this was out of my understanding and how I had previously lived. Now I have total freedom and live in a house and not in a box; I didn't know how to behave as a loving home companion. Now, I'm sitting on the couch and sitting next to her as she touches a small box. With me is my favorite toy and I am happy. This is a lovely life never being in a crate and having my own soft couch and a mistress who always pets me and gives me awesome treats.

It's all going so well. I think of the kids who rough-played with me every time Heather comes to the farm. She stands quietly with my mistress. I keep wanting to play with her because this reminds me of my beginning days, of jumping and grabbing things. They play with me too, in my huge grass yard where we go every day to practice walking. I even went to a place and picked out my own toys. I was so excited that I dribbled on their floor. Nobody seemed to mind; after all, I'm only a rather large puppy. I think there are others doing the same thing because along with a clean smell I detect others. This is so much better. I am learning lots of new things and all this freedom is becoming comfortable.

I have gotten to know the long-legged animals they call horses and I get to visit them. Each one has a different smell and acts differently. The brown-colored one gave me a long sniff and I could tell that she knew others such as me. She has decided that I am a friend and I walk around in her place. One time she walked out of her place, and I quietly followed her while she talked to her other friend. I could tell my mistress was worried because she wasn't supposed to be there. I stood there until she asked me to come outside the gate that was the entrance to my play yard. My friends also used this yard because their smells were there. I stood by the gate waiting for her and she returned and gave me a treat. She is very dependable. I never get in trouble, even when I make mistakes. This is my happy home, and I can be with them all the time.

Today I get to run with my mistress to the big green yard. It is so much fun to stretch my long, growing legs. I know the way and when she calls, I come right away. Today there are several kids near the barn throwing blocks around. Wow. They look like the kids I played with, so I ran right over to play. They were too busy playing with their green blocks and ignored me. I see Heather who is standing quietly with my mistress. I run to them, wanting to play, but they stand quietly, so I immediately sit and get a treat from my mistress. I know this is my forever home because I fit in so well, and they love me so much.

Afterword

It is with change that we are challenged. It is also with profound loss that we step back to evaluate future decisions. Looking back on the timeline of where this story began through the many years until now, it feels like a series of lifetimes, each segment of the timeline having its own direction. Appraising the whole story of all the wonderful animals, people, and places seems unreal. And as an editor commented reading my last book, this must be fiction because all the stories seem fabricated. Upon publishing the book *All for the Love of Horses,* this editor insisted that it be placed in the fiction category. It wasn't until later that this book was placed in the correct category.

I guess the whole series of happenings and finally adding the extensive chapters about the Great Danes, it was inevitable that these stories be written, especially because of the larger-than-life personality of Allie. Her absence made it obvious how much she influenced our life on the farm. Now that I have decided that it must continue, I began in the days after her sudden loss to consider how much she meant to our lives and that the empty space had to be filled with happiness. I'm looking forward to getting Sharlie used to going for romps through the pasture, just like we did with all the young horses and Allie, progressively a little each day so they don't strain young legs and they stay healthy.

It should be noted that as much as we fear loss and its demands of much challenge, when we look back and press forward, we find ourselves in a unique situation of attention and not dwelling on what is missed because we have infused our life with new but different activities. I miss Allie so much and think of her often, but I thankfully now have Sharlie, who walks with me to feed the horses, clean the stalls, and enjoys her own farm to run and play, finding all kinds of interesting things.

As I make my last trip to the barn to feed and check the horses for the evening, it's a joy to see Sharlie happily running around, following me to the barn just as Allie did, and now tired out and sleeping on her couch, or she stretches out next to me while I work nearby on my laptop to finish the next story. It feels like she's still here…perhaps she is.

The Wonderful Support

In life there are always people who by their effort and dedication support our pets. As I think back throughout the time of being involved with horses and Great Danes, with both good and bad there has always been someone who stepped in to help. I called it the act of the good fairy who countermanded the evil fairy from the story of Sleeping Beaty. The good fairy can't change the evil spell on the princess but softens it so that she doesn't die. In my book *All for the Love of Horses,* I recount numerous times that someone intervened to make the outcome less harsh.

It is the many vets who took the extra time to perform more than the physical necessity, who went further because they thought they could be effective, for the quality of an animal's life. All those who helped in the stories in *All for the Love of Horses* and the people who assisted with my dogs made a difference in our lives. It was all the military veterinary clinics; the Loving Care Pet Clinic; Dr. Russell; Nisqually Veterinary Clinic; Dr. Thomas; Dr. Best, who sadly decided to retire; and the Olympia Equine Veterinary Services, with Drs. Grubb and Dailey, and all the dedicated capable vet assistants. Without their help it would have been impossible to make all my beloved pets, lives complete. Besides taking care of health needs, helping a pet make a life's transition peacefully is without words for the owner.

It is also with heartfelt thanks to Allie's first mom, Helene who shared much about her beginnings and whose interest in Allie became the idea for the Great Dane stories. In addition, gratitude to Bill for helping with the recent horse and Great Dane photos, including his relentless devotion to the farm's continued success.

In the many years of having animal companions, there have been difficult occurrences and evil people, but out of all the stories there have been several who cannot change the outcome but soften it. These stories that focus on Great Danes highlight the many kind people who sometimes couldn't change the outcome, but without being asked provided kindnesses that made the situation less hurtful. The end of life is without words but more important is that we are cherished and loved. And they were.

References

Beitman, B. (2022). *Connecting coincidence.* Deerfield, FL: Health Communications Inc.

Bruce Cameron, W. (2010). *A dog's purpose.* NY: A Forge Book.

Dammier, P. (2022). *All for the love of horses.* ID: Iuniverse.

Dammier, P. (2019). *Positive horses.* ID: Iuniverse.

Deutsche Dogge (2019). Retrieved July 19, 2024 from https://www.doggen.de

Reed, Z. (2020). *The Great Dane puppy book, NY: Whistle Books LLC.*

Reed, Z. (2020). *15 things I didn't know until I owned a Great Dane!* Retrieved July 19, 2024 from https://www.greatdanecare.com.

Printed in the United States
by Baker & Taylor Publisher Services